Goodbye
Highland Yankee

Goodbye
Highland Yankee

STORIES OF A NORTH COUNTRY BOYHOOD

by Scott E. Hastings Jr.

with illustrations by Michael McCurdy

Chelsea Green Publishing Company   Chelsea, Vermont

First paperback printing

Library of Congress Cataloging-in-Publication Data

Hastings, Scott E.   Goodbye highland yankee / by Scott Hastings.
    p. cm.
   ISBN 0-930031-17-2 : $17.95
   1. Vermont—Social life and customs. 2. Connecticut River
Valley—Social life and customs. 3. Hastings, Scott E.—Childhood
and youth. I. Title.
F54.H37 1988
974.3'04'0924—dc19
[B]   88-17697
                                               CIP

This book is for Elsie Elizabeth

Contents

Part One
River Towns

Part Two
The Farm at McIndoe Falls

Part Three

Workingmen

Acknowledgements

I owe a deep debt of gratitude to Elsie Elizabeth Hastings for the comfort and support only a very special friend can give. She has been an unfailing source of love, strength and inspiration for more than forty years and throughout the writing of this book. Without her it would not have been written.

I want to warmly thank my parents, Scott and Jo Hastings, who, both visibly and invisibly, figure so large in the following pages.

I wish they were still alive so I could say thank you to my grandparents, Oliver and Belle Hastings, and all the aunts and uncles on both sides of my family.

My three sons, Scott, Alec and Duncan, grew up on these stories and others told by my father and their Uncle Bob. They have often encouraged me to set them down. (Thanks, guys!)

Special thanks are due Lorene De Melo and Fred and Olga Straka of the magazine *Window of Vermont*: Lorene for encouraging me to submit some of these tales to the magazine in the first place; all three for helping me with advice and much good talk in the process of publishing several of them in my feature column, "Scatterings."

I want to express my sincere thanks, for many things, to the following friends who are listed in alphabetical order: Archie Baker, Sherburne, Vt., Jack and Sally Comstock, Hartland, Vt., Orien Dunn, Victory, Vt., Donald Guganig, Monroe, N.H., Bert and Mary Holland, East Corinth, Vt., Leo and Grace Hutchinson, Corinth, Vt., Merton "Jim" Nott, West Hartford, Vt., Ruth Page, East Corinth, Vt., Mr. and Mrs. Arthur Palmer, North Thetford, Vt., Joseph Quinn, Hancock, N.H., Mr. and Mrs. Chester Randlett, Belknap, N.H., Sonny Sawyer, Plainfield, N.H., and Angelina Scelza, White River Junction, Vt.

To four old and dear friends, George Fordyce Ritchie, Springfield, Vt., Maurice Page, East Corinth, Vt., Edward Clay, North Thetford, Vt., and Benjamin Thresher, West Barnet, Vt., who among them taught me to play the bagpipe, ride a motorcycle, and build water tubs—as well as much about running a water-powered mill, hill farming, and country folk—to these four friends I owe a debt of gratitude that runs especially deep.

Last, but by no means least, I wish to thank my publishers Ian and Margo Baldwin for their abiding faith in the book and help and encouragement during its writing, and Susan Weber for her patient and exacting work in editing the manuscript.

Scott E. Hastings Jr.
Taftsville, Vermont

Foreword

I was born in October of 1924 in McIndoe Falls, a village in Vermont's Northeast Kingdom where my paternal grandparents had a farm. Shortly afterward my parents moved a few miles south to East Ryegate. When I was four we moved sixty miles further south to West Lebanon, New Hampshire, a railroad town on the east bank of the Connecticut River. My boyhood years were spent there.

Like millions of other Americans my roots are bicultural, Northeast Kingdom Yankee on my father's side and Provincia di Lombardia on my mother's. I never knew my Italian grandparents. They came to Barre, Vermont, granite capital of the world, just before the turn of the century. My grandfather, trained as a stone carver during his youth in Italy, died of "white lung," the dreaded stonecutter's disease. This was a form of silicosis eventually contracted by most stone workers from exposure to dangerous concentrations of stone dust in the air inside the granite sheds. The last two years of his life he spent in Italy in a vain attempt to recover his health. My mother was only two when he died. By age twelve she had also lost her mother.

My father and mother, and many of my aunts and uncles, were first-rate storytellers. From them I absorbed Yankee lore, some of it filtered through an immigrant experience of life in the northern United States, and many stories of the various adventures undergone by family members.

In 1965, after seventeen years of public school teaching, I received a Northeast Regional Leadership Fellowship from the Ford Foundation. My family and I spent the year at the Research Center of the Museum of Northern Arizona in Flagstaff where I studied folklife and anthropology. At some point during that year I realized that the Yankee world in which I'd grown up was fully as exotic and worthy of examination as any foreign culture, and it had been there all along—I'd just been standing too close to see it. Though I returned to teaching for four years I knew that my real interests now lay in the field of folklife.

In 1971 I wrote Laurance S. Rockefeller proposing that he establish a museum of regional folklife in Woodstock, Vermont. I was hired in 1973 and worked until 1983 as director of the Vermont Folklife Research Project. The traditional regional folklife associated with the antique farming tools and artifacts on display at the Billings Farm Museum persisted, in large part unchanged, straight through the 1930s and early 1940s.

Not surprisingly, the integrating theme of this book is my experience growing up in that folk culture. The pages that follow hold the memories of a man trained to think about the daily lives of a traditional people.

Over a two-hundred-year span the Industrial Revolution cast its wide net over much of Europe and North America. In the flat coastal and inland basins of the United States it caught cities and great shoals of people. It must not, however, be imagined that after a certain date, or period, a uniform degree of industrialization had developed and everywhere settled over the land. The path to an industrialized world was much more ragged than that. In many areas, especially in isolated mountainous regions along its edges, the net did not draw as fine. In such places a few folk slipped through the mesh, continuing to live much as did the subsistence-based country dwellers of the mid-nineteenth century. For these the transition toward life in industrial society was, until shortly after World War II, slower and more idiosyncratic than for people living in the population centers.

This book illuminates the daily life of some who grew up and lived in one such world, which lay the other side of that war. This was the folk stratum of life as it then existed in the little towns and rural countryside in the highlands of eastern Vermont and the New Hampshire border country, between the Green Mountains and across the valley of the upper Connecticut River. It was a world still in the process of entering the age of electricity and the automobile, and it continued to use as prime movers: draft animals, human muscle, and the power inherent in falling water and in steam. As children we saw Gypsies on the road and encamped; smelled fresh hay let down with a hand scythe; watched fields of Indian corn being cut by hand and stooked in long straight lines; and revelled in a real old-fashioned Fourth of July. We rubbed elbows with bootleggers and veterans of nineteenth-century wars; stood beside mountainous black locomotives with steam issuing from their nostrils; heard the shriek of pulleys and belts in an old mill, as they quickened to life under the impetus of the turbine sunk deep in the foundations; and, growing up, we labored at the hard sweaty work that made a drink of cold ale or switchel afterward taste like nectar.

In the 1920s, a watchful eye might have noticed that the self-sufficient ways that sustained the towns and farms of eastern Vermont and the border country wavered slightly and faded just a little. Then they steadied to linger on through the thirties and forties, stuck in place, like a butterfly on a mounting board, by the needle of the Great Depression. For this brief span, regional life retained the incandescence of a well-burning coal fire just before its ashes are stirred with the poker, upon which the glowing mass of red dulls and begins to fall to pieces. For us, though we did not know it, the breakup was coming. After the war the old life, much of it rooted in medieval times, withered away along with the railroads.

Part One

River Towns

Into my heart an air that kills
   From yon far country blows:
What are those blue remembered hills,
   What spires, what farms are those?

That is the land of lost content,
   I see it shining plain,
The happy highways where I went
And cannot come again.

A Shropshire Lad
A. E. Housman

Where We Grew Up

In the 1920s and 1930s, West Lebanon, New Hampshire, and White River Junction, Vermont, were bustling railroad towns. Directly opposite one another on the banks of the Connecticut River, dirtied by years of coal smoke and shabby in places, they were homely, even ugly, towns. Connected by a bridge for trains and another for foot and vehicular traffic, their joint preoccupation with railroading made them appear to the uninitiated eye as one big town. Each, however, possessed a strong sense of identity to which it tenaciously clung. Nonetheless, as railroad towns and river towns to boot, they shared traits in common: one was a well-deserved reputation for toughness. From nearby Hanover, New Hampshire, the Dartmouth College boys, known col-

3

lectively by the residents of the two towns as "pinheads," tested this assumption periodically in the local beer parlors—usually to their cost. West Lebanon kids, when they wanted to see a movie, had to go to the Lyric Theater across the river and they always went with one or two buddies for mutual protection.

Situated as the towns were, in the midst of a rural countryside thickly speckled with farms, they afforded us the opportunity of sharing the very different lives led by farm kids. It was a wonderful place to grow up. If we ever thought about it at all, it must have been with a compound of blind trust and affectionate understanding. It was just where we lived—so familiar a place we accepted it unthinkingly. The largest towns and farms in the region were along the Connecticut where there were flat fertile river meadows. Villages and farms in the adjacent rough uplands of the Vermont and New Hampshire borders ran much smaller.

Coal-burning steam locomotives were a dominant feature of life in both towns. In West Lebanon, the tracks, roundhouse, and machine shops where the trains were repaired, sanded, coaled, and watered were spread out down along the river. The place was marked by a great smoking chimney and the gaunt skeleton of a black crane used to load coal and move ashes. For twenty-four hours every day, the town vibrated to the chuffing of the giant engines proceeding ponderously about their business. The plumes of black smoke rising from their smokestacks caused womenfolk to hang out washing only when the wind blew right, lest the clean clothes become speckled with soot. As children, lying in our beds in the small hours, we heard the long-drawn, mournful hooting of these leviathans as they hauled their rattling strings of freight northward up the valley.

Between the yard and the mountains a half mile away were streets of dwellings perched upon a rising series of riverine terraces. Once, out in the mountains a mile or so behind the town, I stumbled upon the remains of a settlement. A rough forest track suddenly opened onto a field dotted with wild apple trees. The place was pastured and had therefore not grown up to trees and brush. It carried an eerie sense of the people who once lived there. Scattered over the greensward were their cellar holes, the edges of the tumbled stones blurred by moss and grass. Once, a long, long time ago, when river sites were overgrown quagmires and it was common to settle the hills first, the place had been a tiny community.

White River, too, had a repair facility, the Central Vermont Railroad roundhouse, which stood at the north end of the yards. The town, a bustling intense place, was a major railroad center for the North Country. Into it came almost a hundred passenger and freight trains a day. A switching yard in the South End worked around the clock sorting boxcars into strings of freight for final destinations. Down by the river was a hobo jungle and above it, sandwiched between the river and the tracks running alongside White River's Main Street, was Railroad Row: a place filled with large warehouse businesses. To each warehouse ran a railroad siding for offloading freight cars full of lumber, coal, paper, canned goods, fruits and vegetables and—after the repeal of

Prohibition—cases and barrels of wines, ales, and beers. Far more ale than beer was drunk in those days. Ale was the drink of choice in northern New England just as it had been in old England. Beer didn't gain much of a foothold up here till after World War II.

Along Main Street in White River, and on all the nearby streets, were hotels and restaurants of every size and description for the rest and nourishment of train crews and travelers. There was plenty of activity along the street, both night and day. A man could place a bet on the ponies or sit in on a poker game, one of which was known to have gone on, nonstop, for twenty years. Whenever a man folded his hand and left for the trains, another took his place. I remember a neighbor in West Lebanon, a retired railroad engineer with a handlebar mustache, who raised an enormous vegetable garden each year. Early on a summer morning you'd hear him wheezing away, gathering some of the crop to take over to White River in his wheelbarrow. Once there he'd sell the load, then head for the tables and dissipate part of the proceeds on poker and a few ales. About noon the old man would trundle the empty barrow back home, much better for his morning out.

White River had an Italian neighborhood, a street perhaps a half mile long, down alongside the switching yard in the South End. In those times it was solidly populated by people from the south of Italy. Before Repeal, both towns did a flourishing business in the bootlegging trade. The Italians, with their skills in making wine and grappa, and their economically disadvantaged status as immigrants, took to the trade like ducks to water. Once, when my father was helping sort turnips in a storage shed on a bitter November day in the South End, one of the men, when he could stand the cold no longer, said, "The hell with this. Let's go to Fred's house and get some coffee."

Fred White, who lived just down the street, served a lot of coffee: hot and black and laced with 100-proof alcohol. While the men sat nursing the cups in their cold, cracked hands, some Federal men, trying to get something on Fred, walked into the room.

"What are you guys doing here?" demanded the leader.

"What the hell does it look like?" answered one of the men. "We're trying to get warm and Fred offered to make some coffee. We've been sorting turnips in an open shed and we're frozen half to death!"

Fred had the jug well hidden and the Feds, without realizing the evidence was there in the cups, left the house.

Another story, which just missed having a violent ending, involved a Sicilian who got hold of a load of Belgian alcohol in five-gallon tins and stored them in an old shed in South End. Two or three men got wind of it. Occasionally they'd sneak out a tin, transfer the alcohol, refill the tin with water, and put it back in the pile. After a while the Sicilian unwittingly sold several of the tins of water to some very tough customers from whom he was lucky to escape with his life.

By comparison, West Lebanon was an almost sleepy town, though it had its share of characters. Lawrence Tilden, who kept the town cemetery, lived in a big house high above Main Street and used to shoot crows from his back porch. He loved to play chess and he'd sit out there, smoking his pipe and working the moves on a board he'd set up. The crows flew by, just about level with the chessboard, cawing at him. This bothered Lawrence T.'s concentration and that irritated him. When he got mad enough he'd fetch his Hopkins & Allen 20 gauge from the house and lay it across his knees. The next crows that flew by he'd let 'em have it—both barrels. *Broom! Broom!* went the shotgun, followed by the frantic cawing of the survivors as they struggled for altitude. Seconds later came the gentle patter of bird shot bouncing off Main Street. The town policeman drove up in his battered Ford and remonstrated with Lawrence T. but it never did any good. He wouldn't be halfway back downtown before he'd hear the booming of the shotgun again, mingled with the indignant cries of ladies doing their morning shopping amidst the rain of lead.

Except for a gasoline station and a garage, Main Street probably hadn't changed much in fifty years. Sargent's Hotel, a square, green, mansard-roofed building, marked one end and Edson's Bakery Shop the other. In between, a variety of businesses mixed with dwellings lined both sides of the road. Two elderly Greeks lived above one small, narrow-fronted store. Within its mysterious dark interior they sold groceries, beer, fruits and vegetables, and the dried foods and spices of the eastern Mediterranean. I remember the exotic foreign smell of the place when we went in to buy a TD clay pipe or haggle over the two cents return on an empty Moxie bottle, a transaction not always crowned with success for they were hard bargainers.

In the back of an old-fashioned hardware store the owner carried on a tinsmith's shop, which smelt wonderfully of hot solder and oil. Three or four old-timers sat under the Union cavalry saber hanging high up on the wall and if a kid sidled in quietly, and kept his mouth shut, he was allowed to stay and listen. Some of the men were veterans of the Spanish-American War and World War I. One way and another a kid could pick up a fair amount of pretty esoteric information in that backroom tinshop.

At thirteen I served what in an earlier time would have been the beginnings of an apprenticeship to a harnessmaker. Each day after school, I went to his shop and spent two or three hours up to my wrists in neat's-foot oil, cleaning harness. When I wasn't doing that, I cleaned brass, all the while absorbing the inexhaustible fund of lore and stories the ancient knew and was not in the least reluctant to part with. Many of the more old-fashioned men and boys in town (a class to which I belonged by inclination) were in the habit of using profanity as an unthinking part of everyday speech. Some, indeed, had developed swearing into a high art, and it was here in this shop that I began to master the fine points and learned to be comfortable with the practice.

Further along Main Street there was an A&P, and an I.G.A., an independent grocery store. You could call in your order to the I.G.A. and it would be delivered. If you went to the A&P the clerk took your grocery list and put it up for you. In the I.G.A. you could take a basket and wander around shopping for yourself. Some things were still sold in bulk, apricots and dates, for instance, and cookies, which were displayed in big cardboard boxes fitted with glass doors.

One house did double duty as an antique shop and dwelling. There was a pool hall, a dry goods store, a feedstore, two restaurants, and a cobbler's shop where we got our skates sharpened. The drugstore had a soda fountain and booths. It was a favorite hangout both inside and outside, where a wide veranda provided seating for a motley collection of males. Each evening, railroad men, town elders, and a gaggle of boys and young fellows held forth here, the young men looking for action, the older ones content to chat and watch the world go by. At the south end of town was a livery stable and beyond that, on the Glen Road, was the local whorehouse. A Catholic church; a brick-built, wood-heated primary school redolent with the smell of steam heat, wax, and sweeping compound; the post office; a barbershop, whose owner drank scalding hot tea from a saucer each morning at ten; and the Fro-Joy Ice Cream Company just about completed the roll call along the street.

An iceman made his weekly rounds closely followed in summer by children begging for bits of ice. Farmers delivered milk. Ours ran a silver-painted Ford Model A, and once when he stopped at the house a rear fender fell off. I helped him put it back on and was surprised to see it was fastened with simple metal tabs, just like a toy car. There was fungus growing up inside on the roof liner, too. He had good milk, though, despite the inadequacies of his vehicle.

Gypsies sometimes camped in a nearby field. Watching them once, I saw two young Gypsy men burst from a tent, each clinging fiercely to an arm of a white shirt. Yelling wildly, they struggled through the cooking fire, scattering it and upsetting a kettle of stew. When an older man stepped in to end the fight they had already torn the garment in half and each had to be content with the shirt upon his back. The Gypsy women were expert at covering glass jars and vases with tight-fitting skins of woven grass, which they sold door-to-door along with telling fortunes. Some of the grass they dyed a lovely orange color and worked it into the weaving in narrow stripes. It was widely believed by the mothers of the town that the Gypsies stole children. Their arrival on a street was heralded by a scattering of tykes pelting home to Mom as fast as their legs could carry them.

In retrospect, one of the most pleasant characteristics of these little northern New England towns was their human scale. Almost anything a household needed was within easy walking distance. Streets were places in which people lived and interacted. Their comings and goings lasted far into the evenings. A small compass perhaps, but the world was smaller then. Many in the generation before me never got much more than twenty miles from home in all their lives. Few traveled much except railroad men, drummers, and truck drivers, and their range was fixed. Only the Gypsies, hoboes and rich people commonly traveled afar.

Times were hard and most people led lives narrowly circumscribed in terms of money and opportunity. The six-day work week was commonplace and the hours were long. An uncle described his daily round as "going to work with a lantern and coming home with a lantern." There were few labor-saving devices and most tasks called for muscular strength. Yet many people seemed to experience a sense of adventure in simply being alive. In spite of the Depression there was always the chance that tomorrow might somehow be better. And no matter how difficult, when a day's work ended, the hard physical labor made for a sense of accomplishment.

There still was room for individuals who could outdo their fellows in feats of strength and skill and derring-do. A last whiff of the frontier clung to many I knew — like the ephemeral scent of Sweet Grass on a haying day in June.

G-8 and His Battle Aces

A popular activity among kids in the thirties was building model airplanes. We were fans of the World War I fighting aircraft featured in the pulp magazine *G8 And His Battle Aces*. Although one of us sometimes strayed and put together a modern aircraft, most remained loyal to the S.E. 5s, Nieuports, Pfalzes, Fokkers and other, lesser-known, aircraft of the Great War.

We used to wheedle the family dough board from our mothers, put down the plans for, say, an Avro "Spider," cover it with waxed paper, and go to work with razor blade, common pins, and glue. Several days later there emerged a rubber-band-powered scale model resplendent in colorful Japanese tissue covering. With squadron numbers and insignia, plus the red, white, and blue roundel of the Allies, or the black cross of Germany, these models looked like the real thing. Our long-suffering fathers had been without fresh pie during the course of construction. Now mother baked up a storm. There were definite side benefits to the construction of model airplanes.

Jim Slattery, a lanky boyhood chum with a shock of black hair perpetually falling over one eye, built World War I models of astonishing sloppiness. With their warped wings, skewed fuselages and raggedy covering tissue, they still flew better than anyone else's. Seemingly impervious to the laws of gravity, they hovered in extended flight long after the rubber band had run down. The rest of us, who strove for pristine neatness in our models, often saw hours of work perish in a moment as the bright birds staggered in mid-flight, then plummeted to implode against the earth in a pathetic tangle of broken spars and torn paper. Jim's ships never crashed; he knew something the rest of us didn't.

In reading the model builder's magazines that came our way, we learned the city fellows were building *big* model planes. During midsummer of 1937, we decided to have a go at them, too. You chose the aircraft, then sent for plans drawn to the scale you wanted to build to. The balsa spars and sheet for wing ribs, formers, and other structural members had to be bought locally to fit the plan.

Being a builder of good-looking models that never seemed to fly all that well, I took a cautious approach and made a British S.E. 5 pursuit. It had a two-foot wingspan and was powered by a thick rubber band plentifully dusted with talcum powder, said to reduce friction and produce longer flights. No one was more surprised than I when this diminutive fighter proved to be a good flyer.

Harry Swenson built a beautiful Sopwith Camel with a three-foot wingspan. The fuselage was covered in pale brown tissue, the wings and tail assembly in dark orange—the whole doped to a shiny smooth finish. Alas, it never lived to feel the warm sun on its wings. The day after it was finished Harry's old man spotted it and decided he'd take it outside for Harry to fly after school. Like many a father, Horace had stopped for a beer or two on the way home. With diligent care he cradled the Sopwith in both arms and walked through the bedroom door with it—breaking off both wings at their roots. A sad day for Harry, a worse one for his father. Harry salvaged the engine and fuselage, built them into a new ship, and kept it locked in his bedroom.

In making the biggest model of all Jim Slattery abandoned our World War I favorites for an ultra-modern aircraft. He chose to build a Gee Bee Sportster with a four-foot wingspan. A notoriously unstable, blunt-nosed, low-wing monoplane with a huge engine, the ship had already killed several pilots and we somehow felt vaguely betrayed by Jim's choice. Perhaps it was the new challenge that influenced him. Anyway, he bought what he needed at Charlie Poore's hardware store and got down to work. He must have known that with this ship he had a bear by the tail. His quick, impatient work habits vanished for good; he took almost as many pains with its details as if he were building the airplane itself.

15

One day the power plant came in the parcel post. It was like nothing we'd ever seen before. Japanese made, it consisted of an engine, a propeller, and a big brass cannister. You filled the cannister's upper half with water. A mixture of carbide and dry ice went into the bottom. Pulling a ring on top let the water down into the chemicals, generating an explosive gas on which the engine ran. Jim fastened the engine to his dad's chopping block and fired it up. The propeller vanished in a whirling blur of light. The thing sounded like a four-foot boardsaw cutting a hardwood log, not as loud maybe, but just as nasty. We couldn't wait to watch the ship fly.

The last day of October happened to be a day off school. I stopped at Jim's on my way home from jerking sodas at the drugstore. He'd just finished the Gee Bee and he and his dad were admiring it. The smell of his father's cigarette blended with the sharp odor of airplane glue, creating a pungent, not unpleasing, scent. Sitting in a litter of scrap balsa, bent common pins, and bamboo paper, the plane was a thing of matched delicacy and strength. We carried her down to the front lawn to take some pictures. With nothing nearby to give her scale the ship could easily have been real. Dark blue bamboo paper covered the fuselage; the wings were dusty yellow. Her fat, air-filled rubber tires, the pronounced dihedral of her wings, and the oversized propeller gave the Gee Bee a remarkably jaunty look.

"She's a beauty right enough!" pronounced his dad. "She'll be a grand flyer."

"Yeah," said Jim. "We'll try her tonight in the field back of French's Gardens."

When I got to Jim's that Halloween evening most of the neighborhood was already there. His mother and dad too, of course, and his sister and Uncle Eddie, who carried a five-cell flashlight against the coming dark. When Jim came out the door with the Gee Bee, I grabbed the knapsack with the carbide, water bottle, and dry ice wrapped in several layers of newspaper. We started up the road, followed by the excited crowd. It was heavy work getting through the undergrowth bordering the nursery gardens and Jim was hard put to keep the big model from tangling in the bushes. When at last we made the field the sun was almost touching the mountains to the west.

Working against time, we quickly filled the cannister with water and chemicals and pushed it back into its clips. When everything was ready, Jim headed her into the slight breeze and I grabbed the tail as he pulled the cannister ring. A hissing sound issued from the witches' brew down inside as the water hit the chemicals. Jim waited a few seconds and swung the prop over. The engine coughed twice, then caught with a throaty bellow. Pushing the throttle to the firewall, he yelled, "O.K. Let 'er go!"

To wild cheers from the crowd, the ship ran swiftly down the field and took off into the dusk. Black against the rising moon, her stubby silhouette cleared a line of small trees and climbed steeply into the vault of the darkening sky. Higher and higher she went in a series of wide circles, the steady drone of her engine diminishing to that of an angry bee. Uncle Eddie lost her and the dark took her for a few seconds until he recaptured her in the beam of his flashlight. In that brief time, something went very wrong. She was now stand-

17

ing on her tail, clawing for altitude. The clean, even firing of the engine changed to a ragged stacatto and abruptly quit. Faltering, the Gee Bee fell off on one wing, nosed over, and dropped like a stone. Against the moon she looked like a full-sized ship. She hit square on her nose and as we stared in numbed silence, the right wing, strained beyond endurance, let go with a faint "pop" and fell into the grass. A wisp of white vapor leaked from the churning cannister till it fell silent with a last despairing gurgle.

We ran to the wreckage. It was bad. The propeller was smashed, the crankshaft bent, and the fuselage gone clear back to the cockpit. The other wing was busted, too. Jim seemed stunned by the suddenness with which months of work lay in ruins. The crowd stood in a shadowy ring around the wreckage.

"What the hell happened, Jim?" asked a voice.

"Yeah," said the neighborhood wise-guy kid with a nasty chuckle, "it didn't fly very good, did it, Jim? You shoulda stuck to rubber bands."

"Shut up, kid!" said Uncle Eddie and tapped him one with the five-cell, knocking him into the bushes. But the kid was right, even though nobody ever knew for sure just what happened. Jim kinda thought the elevators might have been bent to their climb position carrying the ship up through the brush to the field. Then, when the Gee Bee took off, she simply climbed till she did a power stall and nosed over.

Maybe so. But that's not what the rest of us model builders thought. Somewhere deep down, we all had an edgy feeling the new ship was doomed from the start. Superstition perhaps, but we sensed that in the making of his little, raggedy-ass, rubber-band, World War I fighters that flew so superbly, Jim drew on a kind of careless, carefree magic. Like so much else in our lives, it was fragile, not to be messed with. Under the strains of putting together the big, state-of-the-art Gee Bee, it vanished—jinxed by the new technology.

*In northern New England, two common festivals
retaining a heavy leaven of pagan celebratory
rites were All Hallows Eve and . . .*

The Glorious Fourth

In the 1930s we still celebrated the Fourth of July with passion and élan. True, our activities could not compare to Dad's feat, around the year 1918, of setting off a substantial charge of dynamite on the ledges above McIndoe Falls and smashing almost every window in the village. (He and the other boys had no idea the ledges ran straight under McIndoes right down to the Connecticut River.) The resultant seismic tremors shot through the village like a dose of salts.

Our own efforts paled by comparison. Yet, viewed beside today's feeble observances, it was a wonderful day to be alive. The week or two before the Fourth saw days of frenetic activity as we kids gathered every penny we could scrape up. Piggy banks were smashed with abandon. Even our cherished Indian head pennies, still in circulation as coin of the realm, went into the pot to purchase fireworks. Two of the town's emporiums suddenly and miraculously sported shelves bending under the weight of numerous, gaudily packaged instruments of explosive potential which went to provide our armamenta for the Glorious Fourth.

The store of choice was a narrow, hole-in-the-wall kind of place run by a tough old Sicilian named Joe. Joe stocked firecrackers of every size. These ran the gamut from deadly green five-inchers and yellow two-inchers in dull oily-looking coverings to brightly colored standard inch-and-a-halfs and braided strings of tiny red lady fingers. He sold the ubiquitous sparklers and Egyptian snakes, skyrockets, pinwheels, and Roman candles for the blackness of Fourth of July night. For the day, he offered a teeming multitude of devices with built-in bangs, booms, and gloriously noxious smells.

We used to carefully fold two standard firecrackers in the middle, cracking them and exposing the powder. Then we set them, broken ends facing each other, and touched off the raw powder with a glowing bit of punk. The resultant brief, hissing conflagration, we called a "cat and dog fight." The lady fingers we painstakingly unbraided and set off one by one, for the Great Depression lay heavy on the land. We could not afford to waste them in one profligate, continuous explosion. We were up long before the stars left the sky on the great day. Out on the grass, the dew-silvered cobwebs foretold a fair and sultry day. A few scattered, high-intensity explosions, here and there around the neighborhood, soon told us who was up and ready for action.

21

Jim Slattery's dad loved the Fourth. He always kept on hand a big sack of carbide filched from the railroad. Jim and I'd fill a bag with the coarse tannish-white pebbles, grab the mop bucket, newspapers, a bottle of water and some matches, and head for the field up back of French's Gardens. Once there we'd put a small heap of carbide on the ground and sprinkle it with water. The bucket went on top, upside down with a stick under it to keep an edge up. When we smelled the acrid stench of acetylene we lit a long spill of rolled-up newspaper and touched off the highly explosive gas leaking from under the bucket. The result was a thrilling, drawn out, muffled *whumph,* immediately following which the bucket flew up into the sky and kept going till it was a mere black speck—seemingly as high as the moon still palely gleaming a little above the horizon. We tried this once with a forty-quart milk can and a good big pile of carbide. The heavy can lifted off the ground somewhat ponderously and then kept going. When it reached its apogee it seemed to shift sideways in the sky and Jim and I were hard put, for a second or two, trying to figure which way to run to get out from under it.

After this, we sneaked the much battered mop bucket into Jim's house, ate some Wheaties, and resumed our pursuit of the festive Fourth. The rest of the morning we gathered with the other neighborhood kids for an orgy of detonating the sundry explosives we had managed to accumulate. Unwary passersby, especially girls, dodged and danced among the small brown, paper-wrapped torpedoes we bounced among them. Soup cans burst into shreds under the impact of shiny red cherry bombs' explosions. A granite fence post, with a transverse hole bored through its top, magnified to the roar of a cannon the sound of a five-incher touched off within. Aerial bombs, squat vertical tubes mounted on green-stained wooden bases, threw their charges high into the sky. The resultant clanging, ringing explosions roaring across the heavens brought frightened mothers rushing to doors all along the length of the street.

By noontime we had exhausted our ammunition except for those few fortunate enough to possess the spectacular sky-rockets, pinwheels, and Roman candles reserved for the evening's show. These were packed with chemicals, which upon detonation lit up the night sky with far-ranging showers and streaks of vari-colored lights and trailing streamers of smoke. Lampblack gave red and nitre pink; lycopodium burnt with a brilliant sheet of rose-colored flame; camphor shone dead white and verdigris a handsome pale green.

Between the morning and evening's conflagrant activities, however, there was a one-man fireworks show. The premier event of the day for us kids, it was staged by old man Touhey who timed it to enliven the dull hours of the early afternoon. And until one fatal July Fourth in the late thirties, it had taken on the trappings of an annual event.

Promptly at one o'clock, Touhey, who lived with his wife in a small bungalow at the top of our street, appeared on the bank beside the road above his garden. His yearly burden on this short walk was a tattered bransack full of fireworks. One by one, he set these off. Bangs and booms and crumps and muffled thuds reverberated among the cabbages and broccoli. The serried ranks of vegetables took heavy casualties but the redoubtable Touhey merely grinned and said he planted them only because his wife made him. This was a sentiment with which most of us heartily agreed and we urged him on with cheers.

Touhey was notorious for his method of ignition. He would bring the fuse of the explosive device to the glowing end of the inch-long cigarette permanently pasted to his lower lip. When the fuse lit he would hold the thing in his hand for a moment or two before throwing it, all the while grinning with an air of accomplished bravado. It was well known along the street that Touhey sometimes took a drop more than was good for him. This day, as things turned out, was to be no exception. Halfway through the bag, he extracted a particularly nasty looking piece of work, a dark green firecracker of truly monumental proportions. The thick black fuse looked none too long. To further complicate matters, the thing turned out to be what we in the trade called a "quick burner." Touhey turned to us, his captive audience, and held out the giant cracker.

"Just look at that boys. Old Joe got it special for me. Just wait'll you hear *it* go off!"

Slowly, lovingly, he raised it to the glowing tip of his cigarette. The fuse lit with a splutter of sparks and Touhey held it out casually at arm's length, watching it closely with narrowed eyes. Suddenly it turned on him! The fuse gave a quick *fffsssst* and the cracker exploded with a thunderous *crack!* right in his hand. Loud as it was, it could not drown out Touhey's howl of agony and indignation as the fingers of

24

his hand split open. There followed a moment of shocked silence as he gazed, astounded, at the wreck of his hand. Then Mrs. Touhey (who had been expecting something like this for a long time) rushed out with a towel. She wrapped his poor hand in it and led him, staggering, back into the house. Pretty soon Doc Wilson drove up. When he left, half an hour later, Mrs. Touhey appeared at the door. We were still there, waiting to get news of how Mr. Touhey was faring.

"You boys can have the rest of them goddamm fireworks," she offered. "Touhey's going to be O.K., but he says he never wants to see a firecracker again as long as he lives."

We set 'em off during what was left of the afternoon but the zing had gone out of the day. Things picked up that night, however, when long after dark, Johnny McAdoo had a blue light from a defective Roman candle roll down one shirtsleeve and out the other one. Right after that Charlie Samuels put a big skyrocket into Ora Newton's chickenhouse. Before the fire department could put it out, the smell of spent fireworks had become inextricably mixed with that of roast chicken.

Wild Raspberries and Bread

The summer I was ten we were living next door to Maria in a house we rented from her. She was sixty-three then, a short, strong Italian peasant whose seamed, sun-tanned face and snapping black eyes contrasted pleasantly with the long white hair she wore coiled in a bun at the back of her head. Half a lifetime of poverty and hard work in the old country had so damaged her feet that she wore shoes as little as possible. I remember her always in a shapeless, clean, print dress, with a flour sack apron round her middle if she were working in the kitchen, and broad bare feet.

She came, with her husband Jimmy, from Lugagano in the Province of Piacenza in northern Italy. My mother's parents had come from Lombardia, the next province to the north.

The proximity of the two provinces gave the women something in common—they shared a dialect which they spoke by the hour.

Maria's houses lay on a street at the top of the town—hard against the base of the mountains. The Cinder Lane, a narrow road surfaced with cinders from the railroad, ran downhill between the two properties to the next street. Below her house, at the edge of the lane, Maria kept a chickenhouse with fenced-in yard and on either side of the lane she planted huge gardens, which supplied much of the food for her family as well as a large surplus that she sold. Each spring, as soon as the ground was dry, Eddie LaWare came with a team of horses to plow the gardens and harrow in loads of cow manure.

Afterward, Maria, wearing a tattered straw hat against the sun, raked and hoed all summer long, putting in the crop, watering it, and tending it against weeds. Throughout the summer and early fall she packed loads of vegetables into a child's four-wheeled cart and pulled it daily through the streets, selling the produce door-to-door.

To some, Maria toiling in her fields from dawn to dusk each day or offering, in broken English, the proceeds of her gardens at the doors of the town, seemed an incongruous, even grotesque, figure. They had neither the wit nor the insight necessary to an understanding of her uniqueness as an individual. When she came from Italy she brought with her the cultural baggage of a tiny northern Italian farming village. This she was able to maintain, mostly intact, throughout the balance of a long life. Her life was successful, not only by her own standards, but also by those of the Anglos who had once poked fun at her, for Maria's patient and persistent hard work made her the owner of several good properties in town which she managed wisely and well.

I loved to spend time in her house watching her cook. Her kitchen was a big dark room with a cast iron woodstove and a great wooden table where Maria prepared the food and the family ate. There were pull shades at the windows but no curtains and the house held not a single piece of superfluous furniture. There were no rugs, just well-scrubbed bare wood or linoleum floors. The place had a peculiar, pleasant, clean odor which I have occasionally noticed in Italian homes but never in the houses of Anglos. It was the smell of an alien culture, an exoticism sprung from the activities and materials of daily living: preserved meats hanging from the ceiling, a big wheel of hard Italian cheese in its black rind, spices, homemade pasta, wine and bread, woodsmoke, cooking— these were the obvious ones. And beyond them a range of undefinables.

Terrain, crops, and different kinds and degrees of poverty had a great deal to do with the fact that Italians in different parts of the country ate quite different foods. The north relied on homemade egg and flour pasta, rice, a cornmeal mush called polenta, and used butter as a cooking fat. The mountainous and feudal south used olive oil, hard eggless macaroni, and a variety of tomato sauces. Maria cooked the peasant dishes peculiar to her region of northern Italy, many of them unknown outside her native village.

When, for example, the first peas of the season appeared, she cooked them with rice and broth and a piece of salt pork into a delicious thick soup. In similar fashion, string beans cooked with milk and new potatoes made a simple hearty dish. With bread and a little red wine, either was a filling, nourishing meal. She made her own pasta, the sharp knife flashing in her hand as she cut a thin sheet of dough into even shoestring-like strips that became noodles.

As for ravioli, Maria made a kind I have never tasted outside the walls of her kitchen. She first killed a chicken and saved the white meat. The rest she cooked into a rich broth in a big pot. While it was cooking she rolled a circle of dough out thin and cut a straight edge along the front. The filling was cooked spinach mixed with the finely chopped white chicken meat and cheese. With a spoon, she covered half of the sheet of dough with small mounds of the mixture. Folding over the remaining half, she pressed it firmly down between the little hillocks and cut them into squares with a fluted pastry cutter. The ravioli were cooked in the chicken broth with plenty of handcut noodles.

This kind of Italian food is only found in homes where the old traditions are still alive. Some of the best dishes are the simplest. Of all the wonderful things I tasted at Maria's my favorite was a breakfast she used to give me when we returned from picking raspberries in July on the mountainside back of the town. We went very early in the morning, before the heat of the day. In a cloth sack we carried a bottle of water and a little bread to stay us. Our equipment was simple, a couple of empty lard pails and a huge two-handled kettle. We picked into the lard pails, dumping them into the kettle as we filled them. When we came out of the woods we each carried a handle of the filled kettle and a pailful besides.

Our road took us uphill past French's Gardens to a path winding through a forest and on into rough open pasture. From there a logging road led up to the raspberry patches on the mountain. In the cool and quiet on the steep slope Maria's stories of a peasant's life in northern Italy made the time pass quickly. In two or three hours the containers were full and we came down off the mountain back into the town.

Breakfast after these berrying expeditions never varied. Maria washed her hands and busied herself making coffee and putting milk to heat in a pot. I set the table, placing a deep earthenware bowl, an empty water glass, a spoon, and a coarse napkin at each place. Maria fetched a bulky round loaf of bread with an iron-hard crust from the pantry; cutting big chunks for each of us, she placed them on a plate. While I added two thick wedges of cheese hacked from the wheel, she poured equal parts of coffee and hot milk into our bowls. The result was a steaming hot, pale grey drink which we sweetened to taste. To this day it remains the best coffee I have ever tasted. Then, filling the glasses with homemade red wine diluted with a little water, she pointed to the food and said, "Eat."

Some of the bread we ate with the cheese. The rest we broke into the bowls and ate with a spoon. We finished with a sweet—a dish of fresh raspberries. But the berries weren't really necessary, merely a fillip to the palate. The meal was complete without them.

The Headmaster

West Lebanon had two schools. The first four grades went to
a handsome, old brick primary school down on Main Street.
It had a wood-fired steam boiler and every fall the town
dumped a mountainous load of firewood out on the
playground. At recess all of us, girls and boys alike, helped
the janitor, Mr. Hartley, throw the wood through a window
into the cellar. When it was all in he passed around a bag of
penny candy. On a cold winter's day the pounding clank of
steam making its way through the radiators was a mighty
comforting sound.

When we got so we could write and figure a bit the
teachers rewarded good work by pasting a shiny colored star
to the top of the paper. Gold and silver stars were best but
there were red and blue ones, too. One teacher had rubber

stamps of Palmer Cox's brownies, which she used in place of stars. We much preferred one of the lively little brownies to a star.

Most of the twenty or so youngsters in my grade went all through school together. From fifth grade on we attended school in a building which in the mid-to-late-1800s had been a boy's military school and later the Tilden Female Seminary. It sat in a commanding position halfway up Seminary Hill and in our time it was run by a headmaster of fierce and dominating presence. I have mentioned elsewhere that West Lebanon was a lively town with a few rough edges. Nevertheless, to this day I am not entirely certain whether we, as a product of our time and place, brought out the worst in the headmaster or whether he brought out the worst in us. It was some of both, I suspect.

Behind his back we called him Stub and, as occasion demanded, various epithets that cannot be printed here. He was a short, broad man with gray hair and clear, piercing eyes set under beetling brows. Enormously strong, he had unduly long arms and a nervous habit of shooting his cuffs whenever he was upset or angry, which was a fair share of the time. He ruled by fear. He also played favorites. Athletes, as a general thing, could do no wrong. He used to wrestle the junior and senior football players as a spectacle at the Senior Bazaar. While the boys didn't yet have Stub's heft, they were strong and some of them were as big as he was. He never lost a match.

While Stub's wrestling prowess earned him a kind of grudging respect among the school's male population, he was nevertheless a difficult man to like. For example, in his mathematics classes he had little or no patience with his students who were expected to "get it" the first time around. He did not tolerate questions easily. Once, when a student in our class was struggling with a problem at the blackboard, Stub flew mad and turning to the class said in a scathing voice, "Even a fool could do that problem!" Nope, he definitely was not an endearing character.

He was at his worst as school disciplinarian. His office opened off the main hallway on the first floor. We could easily hear the banging and thumping going on in there as Stub pounded and ricocheted some poor wretch around the four walls of the room. I once saw him in a foaming rage at afternoon dismissal, upbraiding a kid who in a moment of forgetfulness had put on his hat before leaving the building.

"Take off that hat!" he shouted.

The boy, unable to move, could only stand there with a foolish grin on his face.

"Take off that hat, I said!" roared Stub, again to no effect.

Enraged, Stub snatched the hat from his head and fore-armed him into the wall. As the boy slumped to the floor Stub began to put the boots to him. A couple of male teachers dragged him off and held him while some of us helped the kid to his feet. Blood trickled from a cut on his lip. We washed him up in the basement and somebody walked him home. To this day I am unable to understand how the headmaster got away with the things he did, even though many kids who got a thumping at school didn't dare tell about it around the supper table for fear they'd get more.

Some fathers, my own included, once gave him a pretty stern talking to, but it didn't seem to slow him down much.

Stub's attitude invited student reprisals. As long as I was in school there was a kind of guerilla warfare going on. The idea was to get away with whatever you could, as opportunity offered, and be ready to take your lumps when you got caught. A lot went on in that school that perhaps shouldn't have happened simply because Stub's attitude served to put a fine polish on some already hard cases among us. As a result every once in a while Stub took his lumps, too. We derived a rare degree of satisfaction on these occasions. Fifty years later, for those of us who knew him, Stub stories are an integral part of class reunions.

In the high school (as it was before it burned down in my junior year) the science lab was up a narrow, crooked flight of stairs at the very top of the building. One day during a senior chemistry class the instructor left the room. The class took to roughhousing and Stub, who was passing by on the floor below, heard the racket. Stalking silently up the stairs, he burst upon the class yelling at the top of his lungs.

For a brief moment he stood there frenziedly shooting his cuffs, then he made a major mistake. He seized the nearest boy and slammed him into the blackboard, bloodying his nose. Then he threw him down the stairs and started after him. Two football players grabbed Stub and held on. The boy was spunky and he was mad. He ran right back up the stairs and when he saw Stub couldn't get away, he swung one from the floor that connected with his jaw. Stub dropped like he'd been poleaxed. The kid didn't wait for the second round. He ran back down the stairs and kept right on going. He joined the Navy and never came back to school.

But my favorite Stub story is one my brother Bob told me. It happened at the end of a gym class a couple of years after I'd left school. By that time Stub was slowing down a little and had taken to wearing thick, sponge rubber soles on his hall patrols in the hope that their silence and increased traction would compensate for his loss in reaction time. It was a vain hope as things turned out.

Stub had two pet peeves. One was using dirty talk where girls could hear it. Two or three times a year all the boys would be summoned to the assembly hall where he would stride back and forth in front of us, shooting his cuffs while he lectured us on what dirty dogs we were. The gist of his speeches on these occasions never varied. He would tell us in lurid detail what our fate would be if he ever caught us using dirty words in school or, God forbid, touching a girl while passing between classes. He placed great faith in general cleanliness, particularly in the efficacy of cold baths, which he urged us to take as often as possible. By the time he was through we felt like would-be rapists.

His other peeve, oddly enough, and the one that finally brought him to grief, was that the boys in gym classes occasionally hit the ceiling with basketballs hard enough to put dents into it. Once we found out this would enrage him, we made it a practice to put in just enough new dents every week so he'd wonder whether he was indeed seeing new ones or just recounting old ones. Exquisite pains were taken never to make enough to let him be really sure, but

35

sometimes we got carried away and he would go berserk.

Bob and his pal Harry were among the boys who continued the good work. At one end of the gymnasium were two heavy doors with windows in the top half. The doors opened onto a broad platform. From there a flight of steps led down to the main hall. There was a quarter-inch crack between the doors and Stub (who had finally figured out that the ceiling damage was being done when the coach left the gym just before the period ended) had begun to crouch behind the doors and peer through the crack, hoping to catch someone hitting the ceiling.

One day when the coach had left by the rear door to supervise the locker room, Bob and Harry flew down each side of the gym, their hands straight out in front of them, and hit the double doors running hard. Stub's face, though neither one knew it, was pressed tightly against the crack. The doors burst open and Stub flew through the air, ass over tip, across the platform, down the steps, and into the main hall where he sprawled face down—out like a light. Harry and Bob, followed by the rest of the boys, paused not to take thought but trampled the prostrate body of their headmaster in their haste to reach the locker room and safety.

They needn't have hurried. Shortly after they got back to class Doc Wilson and the school nurse took Stub home. When he got better and returned to school he seemed, Bob said, somehow subdued. The rubber soles vanished for good.

October Wine

Each year, during the full of the October moon, Maria's husband Jimmy made *vino di casa*—wine of the house. Good, strong, dry, red Italian wine that he put to age in three squat blackened barrels in the shadows and silence of his cellar. On a shelf above the wine Jimmy kept a box of crooked black Italian stogies. Unlike the wine they were vile. Now and then my brother and I sneaked in and sampled the wine, but only once did we try a stogie. It turned us inside out in less than ten minutes. Jimmy knew what was going on. Sometimes as we came out the open door in the cellar wall, we'd meet him coming up from the garden with a hoe over his shoulder. He'd just grin under his mustache, say hello, and go in and get some wine, which he drank sitting against the wall in the sun.

When I saw the truck come with the boxes of black wine grapes I'd hang around watching, trying to help. I must've been about eleven or twelve when Jimmy asked, "Hey, boy, you wanna help make the wine today?"

"Yeah, Jimmy! I'd sure like that."

"All right. You help stack the grapes and you can turn the press when we set it up. Hang around."

Under Maria's watchful eye, we rolled the empty barrels into the sun and rinsed them with boiling water poured in through the bunghole. Afterward we dragged the wine press out and set it beside the cellar door. Another tub of water was set to boil on the kerosene stove, then used to sluice down the wooden base and round, close-slatted pressing tub into which the grapes would go. The press was built of heavy oak timbers. A pleasant feature, still in occasional use on worka-day objects of the time but unheard of on goods made today, was the profusion of lovely stencilling on its surfaces. Stripes, scrolls, and flowers, confined by the chamfered edges of the wood, wreathed the machine.

A stout platform near the base of the press held the tub. A rim around three sides narrowed to a V through which the grape juice flowed into a wash boiler placed beneath. In the cellar the first barrel, bunghole uppermost, lay on its side in a wooden cradle waiting its burden of grape. Across the top of the press a heavy, cast-iron arch carried the massive, square-threaded press screw. At the lower end of the screw, a thick round swivel piece bore on the wooden "follower" laid in on top of the grapes. The screw's upper end terminated in a round steel casting with four stout, upright "fingers."

"All right. Now we start," said Jimmy. We carried a few boxes of grapes outside, pried off the lids, and began to fill the slatted pressing tub. "Push 'em down good," he warned. When the tub was filled, he laid the follower on the grapes and spun the pressing screw down by hand, as hard as he could. Juice laced with grape pulp began pouring from the narrow spaces between the slats of the tub. Jimmy picked up a heavy, three-foot length of oak polished smooth and bright by countless hands.

"O.K. Now watch," he said. Seizing one end, he inserted the other between two of the projecting fingers and gave the screw a turn. Without missing a beat he lowered his end to catch the next finger in line, then lifted it and brought it down behind the finger nearest him and pulled again. "See?" he grunted, "there's a way to do it. You gotta go down-up—get the stick in front of the far finger and behind the near one—then pull. That way you never hafta stop. It goes fast. The juice keeps coming. Now you try it."

It was a little awkward at first. It went slow and I'd miss a finger now and again. But, like any natural work rhythm, once you got used to it, it went smoothly and pretty soon I could go faster than Jimmy. When the last bit of juice was squeezed from the grapes, a back twist loosened the screw so's to run it up by hand and fill the tub with grapes again. As the wash boiler filled, Jimmy dipped the juice and grape pulp into a pail and filled the barrel through a funnel stuck in the bunghole.

Around ten o'clock Jimmy said, "Hold on a minute," and disappeared into the house. He returned carrying a platter with a loaf of Italian bread, a chunk of cheese, and a bunch of onions. From his free hand dangled a pitcher. Crooking a finger he handed me the pitcher and we went into the cellar.

"Here," he said laughing, and pointed to a barrel spigot. "You know how to work this thing. Draw us some wine." We ate sitting on a bench in the sunshine. With his jackknife Jimmy cut off a thick heel of bread and handed it to me with a wedge of cheese. The onions we dipped in olive oil and salt and ate as a garnish.

"Well, how you like it? Wanna work some more? You're pretty good with that turning stick."

"Sure, Jimmy. I'll work all afternoon if you want me to."

"O.K.," he answered, "maybe tomorrow, too, if we don't finish."

We filled the first barrel early that afternoon, bringing the juice up to within an inch or so of the bunghole, which we covered with folded cheesecloth to keep out insects while the wine worked. We had some more wine and bread and started the next barrel. At day's end, as the shadows grew long, we washed the equipment down and closed up shop.

Next day went all too fast. I had the stick technique down to a science and we filled the third and last barrel before noon.

"She'll be ready to test in maybe four, five days," said Jimmy, thumping a barrel end. "If she's done, we siphon her out into a clean barrel to age. Takes a few months after that till she's ready to drink. You can help me again next year. O.K.?"

"O.K. Jimmy. I'll help you again next year."

"Fine. You're a good man; stick right to it and work hard. You wanna draw a little wine off now and then, you help youself. Your father, too. You tell him."

Well, we finished and made everything clean for next year. Let the press dry in the sun before we put it away. And that was that. Nothing was said about pay on either side. I certainly didn't expect any—it was common for kids to pitch in and help out then. I'd enjoyed the experience of doing a man's work. I'd learned to make wine and got to know old Jimmy a bit more. As with Maria, I could appreciate him as an immigrant whose experience of life had been considerably different than that of most people I knew.

Under the hazy purple hills of Indian summer I helped Maria stack the field beans. When they dried we threshed them out. I helped myself to a little wine sometimes and got a jug or two for the house. It was good wine. I guess the only fly in the ointment that fall was watching Dad go off hunting with his friends. I wanted desperately to go. Teasing finally got him to promise that when I had a rifle he'd begin teaching me to use it. "Start saving your money, boy," he said. The days wore on. Snow came early and we polished the runners of the traverse and got out the snowshoes. We began spending a lot of time sliding and snowshoeing in the woods that pressed against the edge of the village.

Christmas came and we woke to a gray sky with fine hard snow coming down. We went downstairs to the tree to see the presents and Dad said, "There'll be a lot of snow in this one." And there was. Mom put breakfast on hold while the presents were opened. At length we were done and were admiring one another's gifts when Dad winked at Mom and left the room. Didn't think I saw him but I did. He came back carrying a long slim package wrapped in newspaper tied with thin brown twine.

"Open it up," he said, handing it to me. "See what it is."

I read the card. "Buono Natale, from Maria and Jimmy," it said in a crabbed strong hand. I got the twine off, stripped the paper, and there across my knees lay a twenty-two rifle. It was a used one, but like new. A nice little Stevens rolling block, lever-action, with the words FAVORITE and 22 LONG RIFLE stamped into the top of the action. I have it still; it's an antique now. The edges of the walnut forearm carry rows of tiny, neatly cut notches memorializing kills by Jimmy and Maria's sons. I wasn't taking in the details too well just then because I was seeing the new rifle through somewhat blurred vision—still sleepy, I guess.

Later that day I went over to Jimmy and Maria's house for roasted chestnuts and Italian candies. I tried to get out the words to thank them but couldn't. Maria smiled as she said, "S'all right boy. You can bring us a squirrel or a rabbit now and then."

And Jimmy saying gruffly to cover his own emotion, "Here, have a little glass of wine with the chestnuts. It's good—should be 'cause it's what we made. It'sa nice to swap, huh?"

There is a history in all men's lives.

Henry IV
William Shakespeare

A History Lesson

I guess I was about twelve when I first became aware that there is a lot more to history than can be gleaned from the scribblings of scribes, conveyancers, and clericals, writing for and about rulers, generals, great men, and ladies.

My mother, one wintry night in the middle of the Depression, took me with her to have a cup of tea at the house of an Irish neighbor woman named Maggie. We'd finished supper not long before. It was my younger brother's night to help with the dishes, so I wandered into the living room to catch "Jack Armstrong, the All American Boy" on the old Day Fan radio. Dad had dibs on it afterward so he could listen to "Colonel Jim Healey and the News," sponsored by Blue Sunoco. His paper lay crumpled on the floor and a series of muffled thuds and curses, followed by the rattle of coal, gave away his present position—down cellar wrestling with the furnace.

Jack Armstrong wasn't doing much; just slogging along on his way to a pyramid hidden deep in the Mexican jungle. I shut off the set and resigned myself to tackling my history homework. We had to memorize a list of Civil War dates and battles for the next day. Just then Mom walked in. Knowing how much I loved to hear Maggie talk, she said, "I'm going over to Maggie's for a cup of tea. Would you like to come?"

"Sure, Mom. But I've got some history to do."

Most mothers would have taken the invitation back at once. Mine, bless her, merely said, "It'll wait till we get home, won't it? We won't be gone long."

I remember it was a cold night; so cold the snow creaked and chirruped under our boots. We could hear the shouts of the kids sliding over in the lane. We walked fast under the pale light cast by the streetlamps. It took only a few minutes to reach Maggie's and she soon had us settled snug in the kitchen with cups of hot tea and a slice of plum pudding for me.

Maggie asked what was I studying in school and when I told her the Civil War she laughed. "And did you notice how many of the generals and other officers have Irish names? They came over in floods to help and to learn about fighting so's to go back to Ireland and help our own get free of the English."

It turned out that as a young woman in Dublin Maggie had lived through the troublous times of the Easter Rising in

1916. Her brother Jack was in the thick of the guerilla warfare that followed hard on its heels. I suppose my homework put her in mind of him for she told us this tale.

"There was hard times in Ireland then, you know. The English had sent the Black and Tans across to harass and kill. They was mostly English officers from the Great War, though they'd emptied out the prisons and sent that lot, too. They had 'em dressed in khaki with a black belt and that's where the name came from.

"They was in Dublin where we lived, and they carried on all manner of killin's and atrocities. Our brother Jack was in the I.R.A. fightin' them. There was a fat price on his head; Black Jack he was called and he was well known at the time.

"One night the Tans was after him and pushin' him hard. He only just got away into the narrow, twisty, little street where we lived. He come round to the back and scratched at the door and we let 'im in. The Tans blocked both ends of the street and begun searchin' the houses along each side. We sisters and mother had a hidey-hole well hidden under the floorboards in my bedroom and we put 'im down in there. It wasn't long till the Tans reached the house and come burstin' in with their rifles, fixed bay'nits and all. Their officer give 'em orders to ransack the place. They went all through, upstairs and down, bustin' furniture and threatnin' us with our lives.

"But they didn't find Jack, the brutes!" she said as with trembling hands she poured out the second cups of tea. "No, that they did not. Poor dear Jack got away that time."

Then, taking a newspaper from a chest in the corner, she

spread its yellowed pages reverently upon the table among the cups. Along the top of the front page a bold black headline proclaimed, BLACK JACK O'MAHONEY ESCAPES! Then she made me pronounce the family name until I could say it, not like an American, but to her satisfaction.

I wish I knew more about Black Jack and whether he got through the "Troubles" alive or not. Perhaps, like so many others, he did not, for the subject was obviously a painful one and Maggie never spoke of it again. Whether it was the chance combination of the spoken tale and the newspaper headline, I do not know, but something on that long ago night impressed me powerfully that "common" people are not so very ordinary after all.

With pitch and toss and plunge they flew,—
Some skimmed the drifts, some tunneled through;
Then out across the frozen plain
At dizzy speed they shot amain. . . .

The Brownies Tobogganing
Palmer Cox, 1887

The Lightning

By 2:00 P.M., sitting in the warm fifth-grade classroom on a cold winter's day, we could hardly restrain ourselves. We knew the steep roads in our riverside town would be icy and slick—prime for sliding. When dismissal time came at 3:30 we hit the front doors running, and ran the better part of a mile, all the way home. Once there, we frantically changed clothes, bolted a cup of hot cocoa and a fistful of cookies, and made for our sleds on the back porch followed by a shout from mother, "Be sure you get home in time for your supper."

Sometimes we took our snowshoes and went into the wooded hills back of town. Sometimes we put on skis or, if the ice was right, went over to the skating pond in Sam

Lamotte's lumberyard. But more often than not, we slid, slid on a network of steep side streets leading down to Main Street, just above the railroad yard beside the river. It was a long, freezing walk back up to the top of the hill, but when conditions were right you could get a terrific ride. We shared the roads with cars, of course, but in the early thirties lots of people still blocked them up for the winter and there weren't many around. And we could always steer our sleds around them, though Jimmy Slattery once caused a sensation by sliding right underneath a high-bodied, wooden-wheeled truck he took unawares at an intersection.

Dragging our sleds behind us, we fell in with the other kids along the street. By the time we reached Batchelder's Hill at the top of the bad curve onto Farnham Avenue there'd be maybe twenty of us. Breath steaming in the icy air, everybody'd be kicking his feet together to warm them, because we all wore leather highcuts. Highcuts laced almost to the knee and the right one came with a snap pocket holding a jackknife. They were the coldest footgear ever invented, and inside of thirty minutes our feet felt like stones. For the rest, we dressed in woolen long johns and knickers or heavy pants, topped by shirts, sweaters, and a thick mackinaw. Scarves, toques, and mittens warmed the balance.

Most of us owned generic kinds of sleds. These came in three lengths: long, medium, and too short. Mostly, except for the renowned Flexible Flyer—the Pierce-Arrow of the sliding hill—they were too short. Long, sleek, and heavily varnished, the speedy Flexible Flyer had a fierce American eagle stencilled in scarlet and gold across its slatted top. It was famous for sensitive steering and response. The fortunate few who owned them covered the top in three or four inches of thick, soft padding covered with bransacking secured by an intricate web of clothesline rope. Owners of the padded sleds became expert practitioners in the ancient art of the belly bump.

Belly bumping meant standing about twenty feet above the takeoff point of the hill, holding the sled diagonally across your body with both hands. Then you ran as fast as you could (no easy task in all those clothes) and hurled yourself outward into the void and down the hill. You lit on your sled traveling fast, and you picked up more speed as you went along. Illustrations in children's books to the contrary, no one ever rode a sled sitting up except for an occasional lark or to crowd on more kids; you couldn't go as fast.

All of us together could become airborne in about six seconds flat, a hurtling conglomerate of sleds and bodies weaving in and out and passing each other, while continuing down the hill at top speed. The route took in steep hills, sharp curves, a long slide through an open field and, finally, a series of hair-raising turns into a steep pitch that shot the sleds straight onto Main Street. The experience was a kind of Darwinian slide for life; only the fittest made it all the way without incident. That was where the noble art of ditching came into play.

As we hammered along a straight stretch or looped into a sharp turn, another sled was always in the way. You missed him if you could; if you couldn't you ditched him or her, for there was no mercy based on sex. Ditching had its finer points but, in essence, you tried to put the other sled off the road into a snowbank. On a fast sled, a heavier kid could come alongside and steer another sled right into the ditch. Or you could sneak up in back, grab a booted foot and twist, putting the other guy off the road. These were the basic techniques but there were others. Buddies would fly wing on each other, put an enemy ace over the bank with a derisive "ha, ha," and continue down the hill, spreading havoc in their wake.

For sheer capability in ditching, nothing could compare with the padded Flexible Flyers. Heavier, higher, and more responsive, they were the terrors of the hill. Smaller kids, riding the generics, could expect to spend a lot of time in the ditch or over the bank. Some of my pals and I were in this category. I remember once I dragged my sled back onto the road and saw my Dad standing with a grin on his face.

"Got wiped out, huh?" he remarked.

"Yep. Happens all the time," I replied.

Dad looked thoughtful, and then walked off. He and Mother had moved south to West Lebanon from East Ryegate, a village in the lower reaches of the Northeast Kingdom. The old ways lingered longer there and one of them was sliding with a traverse. Outside this region it's called a bobsled, but here it goes by traverse, a word probably derived from our French neighbors to the north. We also called it a "trav'lse," "traviss," and sometimes a "double runner." Its size varied from giant twenty-footers holding upward of twelve people to smaller three- and four-man versions. Any traverse, no matter what its size, consisted of two, stoutly built, low wooden sleds fastened to the ends of a long wide spruce board that often carried foot rails for the passengers. Up front a foot brace projected at each side for the driver's feet. The front runner pivoted on an iron pin, and a half-inch manila rope knotted to holes in its ends enabled the driver to steer sitting up. You could also lie at full length and steer, while a buddy at the back rode shotgun.

Dad got someone he knew up north to build a racing traverse for my brother Bob and me. One night he got home late, walked us out into the shed, and there it was. A real beauty. The runners hadn't been ironed yet but Dad got an elderly blacksmith across the river to do it. The runners he put on were made of half-inch round steel rod.

"These are racing runners, boys," said the smith. "Flat steel slides all over, but round stock bites in. It lets you go exactly where you want to go."

Was he ever right! We painted the traverse silver with a jagged red streak of lightning down the center. Then we took her over to the top of the hill. None of the other kids had ever seen a traverse and they took on something fierce, hooting insults and laughing at it. But they didn't laugh long. Three of us got on sitting up and pushed off with the pack after us. You couldn't get off to a belly bump start with her but you didn't need to—she was *fast*.

Suddenly the kid behind me pounded my shoulder. "They're right behind us," he screamed. One of the Flyers pulled up even and we looked down to see Bud Perry, the nemesis of the hill, grinning up at us. "Bye, bye, fellas," he yelled—prematurely as it turned out. He turned into us as we pulled hard left. Lightning jackknifed slightly, catching him unawares. As one man my buddies reached out, grabbed the side of his sled, and lifted. Bud flew off and went pinwheeling down the icy track. His sled, now bottom side up, caught the runners of the sled behind and within seconds the hill was a logjam of kids and sleds flying off the road in every direction.

The experience of riding a traverse is totally different from the quiet, hissing ride of a sled. The runners make a kind of rumbling noise, hard to describe but never to be forgotten. Manueverable to a fault, Lightning became queen of the hill; nothing could take her. I know because I got a chance to ride the Flexible Flyers, trying to ditch Lightning myself, with their owners on board her. On the last trip that first day, just before quitting for supper, we noticed Dad standing beside the road on his way home from work. I thought he was entitled to a demonstration, so we jackknifed Lightning, putting a couple of nearby sleds off the road. I'd put too much English on her, however, not yet being used to what she could do. We shot by Dad sideways, caught the snowbank, and wound up scattered in the field.

At supper Mom asked, "How did the new traverse go? Is she fast? Do you like her?"

Dad laid down his fork and grinned. "Well, Jo," he said, "I can answer that. I saw 'em tonight on my way home and they went by like the Flying Dutchman. I'd say they like her fine." Then, with a wink, "Prob'ly like her even better when they get so they can handle her."

The Iron Canaries

Dad always was an avid hunter. Much earlier, when we lived in East Ryegate, he hunted a lot with Dick Batten who lived next door and kept some good coon hounds. One day, when I was about four, I was in Mr. Batten's garage with Dad. While they were talking hunting, an oblong patch of sunlight on the floor caught my eye. I followed the slanting rays to a long window in the back wall. Sitting on a narrow shelf across its center, black against the dusty sunlit panes, was a row of small birds. Mr. Batten saw me staring at them. Laughing, he took one down and handed it to me.

"Those are my iron canaries," he said, "They can't fly away. Here, you can have this one if you like."

I was delighted and thanked him. When he and Dad fell to

talking again I looked closely at what I had. The bird was a little casting, perhaps 3 ½" long. While it did somewhat resemble a canary, it could as easily have been a sparrow or almost any other small bird. And it wasn't really black but a dull yellow and of a peculiar battered appearance. I had no idea then what the birds were. Some years later I discovered they were twenty-two rifle targets. You set them up along a narrow board placed in front of an earthen bank to catch the bullets and shot them off—if you could.

After Christmas, the winter Jimmy and Maria gave me the twenty-two, Dad began to teach me to shoot. He was strong on safety. By the time he got that drilled into me to his satisfaction it was getting on toward spring. We never used paper targets—we went out to a sandpit and shot tin cans. The first thing I learned was that my right eye had been virtually blind since birth. I'd compensated so well none of us ever knew it, but I had to learn to shoot left-handed. Even with the one eye I got to be pretty deadly with a twenty-two. When I was able to hit a can ten times out of ten at fifty feet, Dad began putting them out further and further and I kept right on hitting them. Then I went to finishing school at the local dump.

Lots of folks brought a rifle along when they went to the dump. There were usually half a dozen or so boys and men standing around the top edge shooting rats down on the steep face. The trick was to stand perfectly still and watch. Pretty soon a big gray granddaddy rat would venture out and make a run for it across the twisted frames of wrecked cars and smashed refrigerators. I learned to swing the sights onto him fast and squeeze the trigger. The twenty-two long rifle slug would send him flying. Besides getting some good practice in the fine points of shooting, we helped keep the thriving rat population in check.

One night that summer, Dad asked whether I'd like to go with him on his trip next day. He was a salesman for the Twin State Fruit Corporation, and he covered a large territory in the country, up north along both sides of the Connecticut River. I immediately said yes. He didn't take my brother or me often. His hours were long and by day's end we'd get pretty tired.

Early next morning he gassed up his car at Twin State, picked up the day's prices and off we went—traveling out into the big world and into strange towns. Children hardly ever got very far from home then and it was a real treat for me. I met some of the men he sold to and even had lunch in a restaurant. At the end of that long summer's day we circled a mountain away out beyond Orford, New Hampshire, and took a steep dirt road up a narrow valley where a shabby general store perched at a crossroads. There were some cars parked in front near a pair of gasoline pumps, and a white church stood across the road, and that was it. The store sold everything: groceries, dry goods, horse blankets and harnesses, patent medicines, tinware and tools. Boots and snowshoes hung from the ceiling. Three or four two-man crosscut saws and a couple of bucksaws dangled from wall pegs above some axes and peavies stacked in a corner. There was even a walking plow out in back. The storekeeper, a kindly, white-haired gent wearing wire-rimmed glasses and a white apron, said, "You look like you could use a tonic, son."

Lifting the lid of a wooden tonic cooler full of bottles sitting in ice and water, he pulled out a dripping bottle of Mission Orange and handed it to me. I thanked him and drank it slowly, leaning against the cooler while Dad wrote down the order.

Afterward we drifted out behind the store. A bunch of men dressed in bib overalls, blue workshirts, and battered felt hats stood looking at something down at the far end of the yard. Dad seemed to know them all and stood around joking and laughing with them. The sun had by now dropped well down toward the mountains and it was getting harder to see. Squinching my eyes, I looked, too. With a sinking feeling, I made out a long line of "Dick Batten" canaries lined up on a board set on a couple of sawhorses. They had come back to haunt me. My twenty-two suddenly appeared in Dad's hands and he pointed to the yellow birds.

"June," he said (he always called me June and right then, in front of that crowd, it didn't help any), "just see how many of those little birds you can knock off that board."

I'd like to be able to say that I was cool under pressure but I wasn't. It was getting pretty dusky, and I was tired and not seeing as well as I should for that kind of shooting. Also, I knew, with a sickening, sure knowledge, that money was about to change hands one way or another. I forgot everything I knew about shooting. I don't think I hit even one. When I finished there was a deathly silence. Dad was stricken, besides being out some cash he couldn't afford to lose.

The storekeeper who owned those birds put his arm around my shoulders and said, "Well, kid, what the hell. Nobody could shoot good in this light."

Which was nice of him but didn't do one single thing to stop my knowing I should have shot the ass off every one of those little iron bastards.

It was a pretty quiet ride home. When we got to Orford, New Hampshire, Dad pulled in and stopped at The Elms, even though it was late. He got me an ice cream soda while he and his old friend, Henry Carr, had a stiff gin apiece. Dad needed it more than Henry. He tried hard to cheer me up on the way back home. Whatever he said was wiped out of my mind by the dismal fact I'd let him down after he'd bragged me up as a Deadeye Dick.

The next Sunday we went rat shooting at the dump and I ran up a string of twelve—just like that. Trouble was, there was no one there to see it but Dad and me and a couple of other ratters.

Tweed said to Till,
"What gars ye rin sae still?"
Till said to Tweed,
"Though ye rin wi' speed,
And I rin slaw,
Whar ye droon ae man,
I droon twa."

Dialogue of the Rivers
Anonymous

Inland Yankee Working Boats

The Connecticut River, as it flows between the twin towns of West Lebanon, New Hampshire, and White River Junction, Vermont, was tamed in the 1950s by Wilder Dam. But when I was a boy, fifteen or twenty years after the last of the long log drives, it was a stretch of river to be reckoned with. Its black waters were swift, deep, and treacherous. Once we watched a carnival high diver go off the bridge between the two towns. He did it as a stunt to drum up attendance. Poised on the railing, looking down at the roiling waters below, I don't think he wanted to go but there was a good-sized crowd and they started to catcall. Finally he dove. He didn't come up for a long time. We finally spotted him swimming to shore far downstream of the bridge. Drownings were no uncommon event in those two towns.

My first experience of being on the river came when Dad borrowed a rowboat and took my brother and me fishing below the ancient canal locks at Lower Falls in the northern outskirts of West Lebanon. We went down through a pasture into dark hemlock woods, clambered over the monumental stonework, and found the clumsy boat tied to a tree below the rapids. The river, having dropped over thirty feet in less than a mile, narrowed here and poured through a steep, ledge-filled chute. One could see the jagged stone sheeted under the pounding green water. Snags, sticking free of the surface, atomized the beating current into an expanse of rough broken water topped by blowing foam and mist. The water's roar was so loud we had to yell to hear each other. A slender eddy ran up almost to the head of the rapids; in time I was to become well acquainted with it.

I don't recall whether we caught any fish that day, but my chums and I had found a new field for exploration. Now our hikes took us up to the old canal locks where we climbed and shinnied over the high thick walls. Once, a long, long time ago, river boats detoured the rapids here on their way to Barnet sixty or seventy miles north. Though the wooden gates were long gone, some of the big, hand-forged pins from which they'd hung still protruded from the stone walls. About this time I made up my mind that someday I'd have my own boat and shoot the tumbling waters in that stone-choked channel by the locks.

I finally got the boat because of three things that happened in the summer I was fifteen. In talking with my grandfather, I learned he'd gone on the log drives down the Connecticut.

In the process he learned how to handle bateaux, those thirty-three-foot, awesomely graceful rowing boats, which were the equivalent of pack horses on the drives. He told me a little of how the boats were constructed (he may well have had a hand in building them, for he was an expert carpenter) and that they each carried up to a ton of boom chain and the bedrolls and equipment for seven men. And he told me how, when on its long journey down the river the drive encountered a dam, he and another young fellow sometimes rode the bateaux straight through the sluiceway, dropping with a crash into the river below, to avoid the heavy work of portaging, or as he put it, "foraging," the boats around the dam. I told him I intended to build a boat and put it in the river.

A week later Gramp sent down from his farm two long boards of eighteen-inch wide, clear white pine. They came from a big tree he'd cut years before, and I think he kept them to make a boat he never got to. Not only did I earn money that summer to build them into a boat, I also discovered the perfect plans in *Deep River Jim's Trail Book*. Only a few can now recall Deep River Jim. I think his was the official handbook for a boy's magazine outdoor club. In it, among a maze of tricks and information for living in the out-of-doors, were the plans and instructions for building a thirteen-foot Maine logging skiff named *Yankee Pine*. In several respects she was put together much like a bateau. Deep River Jim, if he ever really existed, almost certainly had firsthand experience with the drives.

Construction techniques for both boats differed sharply from those used in today's high-tech world of wooden-boat building. *Yankee Pine* and her big sister, the bateau, were fashioned to the beat of a different drummer. Work boats made for hard seasonal use on lakes and rivers, neither was expected to last forever. They were folk built in a few remote villages in the Northeast Kingdom, the New Hampshire North Country, and down Maine. Both boats were constructed using local materials and simple hand tools, according to the dictates of long-established patterns. They were roomy and beautifully shaped with deeply flared sides. The bateau, unlike the skiff, which had a square stern, was double-ended. Both craft had a long, slanting overhang at the bow, and in the case of the bateau at the stern as well. The double overhang combined with the flaring sides to give the bateau a short, narrow bottom for its size. It could spin on a dime and leave change. And it could be rowed and poled backward, as easily as forward. Both craft were exceptionally handy, with outstanding strength and stability in the rough, often stony waters of northern rivers.

When the paint dried on *Yankee Pine*, I moored her to a heavy log-boom ring set in a ledge long ago by the river drivers. She went like a dream, fast and maneuverable. I rowed upstream toward Lower Falls and a long spell of learning about the vagaries of the river. Soon the center of the river began to surge and boil. Some hard pulling at the tail of the rapids worked the skiff up into the eddy close to their head. Only a few feet away, the current roared past in a maelstrom of tossing waves and resistant rock. Knowing if I hesitated I'd never do it, I slanted the boat slightly downstream and took a strong pull at the oars. The bow caught a wave, shot into the air, and slammed down hard in a trough. Flashing over a submerged ledge, she went pitching and tossing through the chute. *Yankee*, now seeming very small indeed, was responsive to the slightest touch. I found it possible not only to miss the standing stones and sunken ledges but eventually increased the thrill of the ride by coming within inches of them. With practice it even became possible to go stern first, allowing one a splendid view of the tumultuous waters immediately downstream.

I spent many happy days and nights on the river in that sturdy boat. By the time I left home *Yankee* was pretty well worn out. I sank her at the foot of the Falls to avoid the ignominy of letting her rot in the field where she had stayed in winters past.

Part Two

The Farm at McIndoe Falls

Lone stands the house, and the chimney-stone is cold.
Lone let it stand, now the friends are all departed,
The kind hearts, the true hearts, that loved the place of old.

Dear Days of Old
Robert Louis Stevenson

Homesite

Gram and Gramp owned a good-sized farm in McIndoe Falls, Vermont, in the southern edge of the Northeast Kingdom. Their village was sixty-five miles north of us. In the late twenties and thirties, that was almost east of the sun and west of the moon. Even so, we managed to get up to the farm three or four times a year.

The farm buildings sat just inside the edge of the village. The front of the white house, with its fluted porch columns and ceiling-to-floor windows, was separated from Route 5 by a broad lawn. Nobody used the front door in this part of the world so when we got there Dad pulled round into the dooryard at the rear of the house. We went in through the back porch to the kitchen, a long room of indeterminate color. On its outside wall, by the windows, was a black cast-iron sink with a tap for spring water. There was no hot water tap; hot water was dipped from a reservoir in the stove as needed. There were curtained shelves underneath the sink and work counters at either end where Gram lined up the kerosene lamps while she trimmed the wicks and cleaned the chimneys with a twist of newspaper. Across the room was a black, cast-iron cookstove; on it a spatter-blue enamel coffeepot simmered from morning till night. Here, when all the family came home for a weekend, say during haying time, Gram and her daughters-in-law did the cooking. They always began breakfast by making stacks of toast. Out came one of the stovelids and a toasting rack was put over the glowing coals. When the bread had browned, a little crank at the top of the device swung the untoasted sides in to face the fire. With this rig a person could toast four slices of bread at a time, buttering them with brushfuls of melted butter from a pan on the back of the stove.

After a decent interval spent greeting Gram and Gramp and saying hello to Indian Joe, the hired man, my brother and I headed straight for the pantry. It was at the far end of the kitchen, just beside the door leading into the spring shed and Gramp's favorite chair by the woodbox. Once inside the pantry we'd pause to take it in. Behind curtains, on shelves fitted to the far wall, were shiny tin milk pans with thick yellow cream rising in them for the making of butter. Other shelves held the biggest assortment of pies, cakes, cookies, and doughnuts I ever saw outside a bakeshop. One fat tan crock contained thick, oblong molasses cookies marked with dark stripes put on by means of a secret known only to Gram. Beside it were jars of date- and raisin-filled cookies, sour cream cookies, caraway seed cookies, gingersnaps, and gargantuan oatmeal cookies studded with raisins. Not for us the bland, cardboard-like, color-and-flavor-added discs that pass for cookies today. Two shelves held only pies—rhubarb, cherry, custard, mince, apple, strawberry, and lemon—always eight or ten. On another shelf were ranks of cakes covered in chocolate or with Dad's favorite thick butter frosting laced with maple syrup and butternuts. Jars of wavy green glass held raised doughnuts, regular doughnuts, and doughnuts placed in a bag and shaken with sugar right after frying. The breadbox was stuffed with loaves of homemade bread. A big jug of fresh cold milk, and one of buttermilk, stood handy with a crock of homemade butter in the icebox. Under the counters were Gram's flour barrels, and the farm's sweetenings: a molasses jug, a tub of soft maple cooking sugar, and a box of hard maple sugar for candy.

We'd pour a glass of milk and start on a wedge of pie while deciding what to have next. Gram knew to a nicety just how much a kid could eat without foundering before supper. Pretty soon she'd come in and chase us out to the barn to help the menfolks. In company with our cousins, we'd still manage to visit the pantry several times a day; in a weekend we could put quite a dent in Gram's array of comestibles.

At the end of the kitchen, a door led into a string of connected spaces under one long roof. First came the spring shed with its round wooden tub full of tooth-numbing water. A tin dipper hung from a nail for anyone who wanted a drink.

An open doorway led to the woodshed and beside it a stair climbed to the attic. The last room was a workshop with the tools and workbench of a master carpenter. As a youngster Gramp had lived for awhile with the Shakers and they taught him carpentering. Carpenter, mason, and farmer—those were his trades.

The farm's square red barn lay behind the workshop close to the edge of the dooryard. A lane out back of the house brought the cows into the barnyard from the hill pastures to the south. In a bank of sand, up back of the barn at the edge of the woods, Gramp and Dad sometimes made beanhole beans, just the way Gramp had seen them cooked on the log drives down the Connecticut. Here, too, was the icehouse where the ice, cut by hand on the river each winter, was stored. We dug the heavy cakes from the sawdust and, with a kid on each handle of the tongs, staggered with them down to the milkhouse. After washing off the sawdust, we broke them up and dumped the pieces into the water tank where Gramp set the forty-quart cans of milk against train time next morning.

To the barn came the store of hay, cut on sunny days, from river meadows a half mile away. Clinging to pitchforks stuck deep in the hay, we rode on top of the towering load, high above the backs of the two stout horses pulling the big creaking wagon. Gramp's was an end-door barn, built against a rise, so the Belgians could pull the load of hay up a ramp onto the haymow floor. We pitched it off by hand onto a rough floor above the tie-ups and down into deep bays on the opposite side of the barn. When the mows were filled level, the men pitched upward stacking the hay clear to the eaves. Years when the crop was especially heavy, some of it was pitched even higher, onto scaffolds on the high beams: heavy work in the hot, dusty immensity at the top of the barn. Just as the kitchen (or for us kids the pantry) was the heart of the house, so was the barn the focus of the farmsite. Together they formed a constellation of hard work and fascinating activity; a fixed point around which the seasons and the lives of the family revolved.

Haying Time

In late May or early June, Gramp began to hay the farm in McIndoes. Haying called Dad home. Off we'd go, early on a Friday night, following the river north. The ride seemed to take forever, but at last we'd hit East Ryegate and know we were almost there. If the milking wasn't done we'd go into the barn with Dad while he helped Gramp and Indian Joe finish up. Sometimes Uncle Bill would be there, too, perched on a three-legged milking stool, the jets of warm milk rattling off the bottom of his pail till it began to fill. This was all hand milking, of course, and there'd always be a couple of farm cats sitting beside Gramp silently begging. He'd wink at us and then speak to the cats. They'd half rise up on their hind feet and open their jaws wide as Gramp squirted a stream from one of the teats straight into a mouth.

Sometimes he'd let 'em have it right in the eyes to keep them on their toes, then he'd laugh.

Next morning Uncle Rinx would show up with Aunt Louine who, because she was short and broad, he jokingly called "Stub." Our McIndoe Falls cousins, Sis, Lloyd, and Francis, came to help and a large, lively crew sat down to breakfast after the milking and chores were done. After breakfast, while the men hitched the team of Belgians to the hayrack, Gram made up a batch of cold switchel in a milk can. Her receipt was: one gallon of cold spring water, a quart of apple cider vinegar, two cups of molasses, four table-spoons of ground ginger, and two or three handfuls of raw oatmeal scattered on top.

She multiplied this as many times as needed, never failing to add the oatmeal, which gave flavor and consistency to the drink and protected against heat prostration. The receipt varied from region to region and many people never knew about the oatmeal, which was a trick of the local Scottish population. Switchel was pleasant to drink and a great thirst quencher; in the intense heat of the hayfield we drank copi-ously from the sweating can. I must add that the men did not rely solely on Gram for their drink; they made various stealthy preparations on their own, which involved a stumpy stoneware jug sunk in the icy water of the milkhouse tub.

When the back of the wagon was loaded with pitchforks, scythes, and a couple of bull rakes, and the front with men and kids, we were ready and Gramp clucked to the team to go. His little cow dog, Laddie, came with us, lagging in the shade under the wagon. The way led along the main road for perhaps a half mile, then cut sharply to the left following a dirt farm road down to the gently rolling hayfield beside the river.

Almost from the beginning of colonization, English and European grasses gained a foothold among progressive farmers in favored regions where they would grow. Among the ones Gramp cut were the red and white clovers, bluegrass, orchard grass, and native herdsgrass (timothy and foxtail). Herdsgrass and red clover, sown together, became a standby. As Dad once told me, "Timothy and red clover, that used to be a big crop. In the old days they'd have fields of nothing but timothy. There isn't any hay in the world that is better than timothy for a horse."

Redtop was another grass that furnished grazing and a moderate amount of hay on the thin, sour soils of northern New England. There were some strictly local hay types, too. When Dad was a boy a fine hay was cut on two big islands in the Connecticut River near McIndoes.

"They used to call it island grass," he said. "Each island had a big barn on it and they filled them with the hay. Then in the wintertime we'd go over there with a stationary baler and bale it and sled it across the river on the ice."

As soon as we reached the hayfield my cousins took off their shoes and worked barefoot all day. Not to be outdone, my brother and I did the same. We paid for it; after a day running barefoot on the coarse hay stubble, our soles were so sore it hurt to walk.

Gram knew it and after we'd taken our bath that night she got out her big red "medicine box." Opening it she removed a round tin box of Rawleigh's Antiseptic Salve—a sovereign preparation sold door-to-door to farm and village wives. It was a product in which she placed great faith. On a mustard yellow background covered with gold scrollwork, a handsome circular red band bore the legend, HIGHLY MEDICATED. Within the red band, in a heavily ornamented circle, was a picture of Mr. Rawleigh, a calm, studious-looking man with a handsome white mustache, round collar, and tie. Through some trick in the printing he stared with level gaze straight into the eyes of the user. "Here," he seemed to say, "is a medicament for all." Gram spread it thinly on our feet and made us rub it in well and wear socks to bed. Magically, the burning soreness vanished by morning.

Another of Gram's cures had to do with stepping on a nail. I remember the dull throbbing ache to this day. On a farm this was a serious injury due to the threat of lockjaw. If the nail had not penetrated too deeply she bound a piece of salt pork, or a clean rag full of Fels Naptha soap well mixed with sugar, to the wound and let you go about your business. If the nail had gone well into the foot she made up hot flaxseed poultices in cloth bags and you were out of action. You laid on Gramp's couch in a corner of the parlor and whenever the poultice cooled she'd apply a hot one from the supply in the kettle on the stove.

Haying the way Gramp did it in the 1930s was pretty old-fashioned. Though he drove a car, he would never allow a tractor on the farm. He let the hay down with a horse-drawn mowing machine, and began to cut early in the season because he wanted to cut a second crop called rowen. Also, it was important to cut hay early before it became woody. The mowing machine saved considerable work. In Gramp's youth hay was cut with the hand scythe. A line of men stepped off, one after the other, swinging their scythes in eight-foot arcs. Each man's cut lay flat, the stalks pointing in the same direction, in a layer called the swath. We still use the word swath in describing hay downed by the mowing machine.

Once cut, hay was left to wilt in the swath. It had to be as dry as possible before being stored in the barn lest it burst into flame through the dreaded phenomenon of spontaneous combustion. As soon as some of the moisture had evaporated, the hay was shaken out and turned bottom uppermost to speed drying. Not owning a horse-drawn tedder, which did the job quickly and easily, Gramp did it by hand, using a hand rake or pitchfork to toss and upset the hay.

When the sun and wind had dried it, the hay was gathered into windrows stretching the width of the field. Gramp used a dump rake for this task. As the horse went along, the driver stepped on a foot pedal raising the rake's spring tines and releasing the hay. Dumping the hay at precisely the same spot each time left the field covered with even lines of fluffy windrows.

In a dark corner of Gramp's equipment shed hung an antique wooden rig he called a "shinbreaker" or "flopover rake." Up to the Civil War, and for a good while after, some local farmers raked their hay with this "machine." It was nothing more than a stout wooden bar with a wide handle fastened to it. The bar was pierced with rows of elongated wooden teeth and had a set of shafts for the horse that pulled it. When the teeth filled with hay the farmer lifted the handle and the ends of the front teeth caught in the stubble, flipping the bar over and releasing the hay. The name "shinbreaker" came from the nasty propensity of the device to administer a smart crack across the farmer's shins as it flopped over.

Near fences, trees, and big stones, the mowing machine and dump rake couldn't work in close. Gramp always cut these out by hand and raked the hay onto the field with a bull rake, its teeth a good sixteen inches long. We also used the bull rake to clean up the hay scatterings left by the dump rake.

During the afternoon of that first day we pitched the windrows into beehive-shaped piles called haycocks, each covered with a light canvas haycap if it looked like rain. Farmers who had no haycaps raked out the top of the cock into a kind of thatch to shed water. Next morning the haycocks were pitched out flat again and left to dry, with occasional shakings out, the rest of the day.

As soon as the hay "rattled" when handled, it was dry enough to load on the hayrack, a four-wheeled wooden wagon that carried loads of hay seemingly piled up to the sky. Gramp's wagon had a low rail fixed along both sides with pointed hardwood stakes set in it to help lock the load. One of our McIndoes cousins drove it around the field with a couple of the men on top to build the load. Some men could build a load of hay and some never caught the knack. Dad and Gramp were experts. They took each forkful, as it was pitched up by the men on the ground, and placed it on the load in such a way that it locked the load together as it was built.

The men on the ground separated the windrows into "tumbles," which they pitched up to the men making the load. A tumble was made by taking a pitchfork and separating a long rectangle of hay from the windrow. Its length depended on the mass, or heft, of hay. The men mentally divided the length into quarters, then folded the end ones back onto the middle. This reduced the length of the rectangle by half and doubled its thickness. One end of this piece was then folded back upon the other to form the tumble, a rough square four thicknesses deep. A pitchfork was thrust into its middle and it was pitched up to the men on the hayrack.

Haying was a time of intense, hurried work for "hay has to be made while the sun shines." A hint of rain sent everyone scurrying to load the dried hay and draw it to the barn; a heavy rain could ruin the crop as it lay in the field. At the end of the day there were still the chores and milking to do. It was no easier for the women who carried on the regular work of the household and cooked as well for the extra helpers. Each summer haying came to an end, accompanied by a collective sigh of relief from all hands.

Sing a song of Sixpence,
A pocket full of rye,
Four and twenty blackbirds
Baked in a pie.

When the pie was opened,
The birds began to sing;
Was that not a dainty dish,
To set before the King?

Mother Goose

Pigeon Pie

Centered on the roof peak of the barn sat a big cupola—its four louvered windows facing the points of the compass. From the ridgepole, dozens of pigeons looked down upon the roofs of the village during the daylight hours. When night fell they entered the cupola and slept perched among its beams. Someone, a long time ago, had nailed squares of heavy, rolled-up canvas above each window. Secured by ropes leading down to a cleat on the high beams, they could, by loosening the ropes, be dropped over the windows, thus trapping the pigeons.

In the twenties and thirties when we were young, one of the good things of life was pigeon pie at my grandparents' farm in McIndoes. Once or twice a year, often in the fall, we'd drive up and find Dad's brothers and sisters there with their families. Cousins raced about greeting each other and there was an undercurrent of excitement the whole day. We visited the team of big Belgian horses Gramp kept, looked in at the cows, and jumped in the haymows. When we grew hungry we raided Gram's pantry for cookies and milk. And when chores were done that night we went in to the long dining table and sat down to supper.

By now, word had leaked out that pigeon pie would be the featured dish for tomorrow's Sunday dinner. This meant we would be pressed into service during a pigeon hunt that night and could stay up till all hours. Soon after supper we excited children gathered in the yard while the men enjoyed a last smoke. As soon as it was dark we filtered quietly into the barn, climbed the stairs, and entered the hayloft floor. Barn lanterns, lit and secured to pegs, cast a pale yellow light that spilled out over the mows down on to the rough floor below. High above, the heavy timbers supporting the roof melted into a black shadowy void. Our oldest cousin, "Bull," almost a man grown, climbed up to the high beams and let go the ropes holding the canvases.

Now Gramp, Dad, and Uncles Buzz, Bill, and Rinx were about to climb the beams into the darkness. Eventually, far up in the roof's structure, they would reach a ladder leading to the cupola. Each had a short club fastened to his belt and Gramp carried a lantern as well. To me they seemed like so many Jacks climbing the beanstalk that disappeared into the lower reaches of the sky. Small wonder they paused on the floor for a fortifying tot out of a black bottle Gramp pulled from a cubbyhole. As the last man climbed up into the shadows we cousins stationed ourselves in the haymow and on the floor. As we waited we observed the men's progress by the faint glow of their lantern as it ascended ever higher among the web of beams. Higher and higher it went till at last it was lost to sight—they had pulled themselves up into the cupola. Here they quietly took up positions on a narrow plank platform built around the sides. The cupola's center was open to the barn floor forty feet below.

We heard a sudden commotion as the men struck at the roosting pigeons with their clubs. The birds, frantic to escape, found their way blocked by the canvas curtains and flew desperately about, beating against the interior of the trap. The men, yelling encouragement to one another and hanging on with one hand, leaned out over the depth, striking at the birds. A rain of dead and injured birds began falling. Some fluttered down; others dropped like stones. Our job was to mark where they fell, chase them down and wring their necks to put them out of their misery, then toss them into a heap on the floor. This we did with enthusiasm. Only afterward, while placing the soft, warm bodies into a basket for transfer to the house, did we feel any pangs of sadness and these were short-lived as we anticipated the feast to come. I remember one pretty brown and white bird had a tiny metal cylinder fastened to one of its legs. Inside was a slip of paper with a coded message, which no one could decipher. It may well have been a bootlegger's bird carrying the news of a shipment of booze from Canada.

After the hunt the grownups sat catching up on family

news while they plucked and dressed the birds. We rose early the next morning to a high activity level in the kitchen as Gram and our aunts cooked breakfast and began preparing the huge pan of deep-dish pigeon pie, which would be served with light, delicately browned, baking powder biscuits floating on the gravy. Indeed it was a dish dainty enough to set before a king and we did it ample justice when we sat down to table late that afternoon.

The tailor took out needle and thread and stitched her together again. The bean thanked him in the most elegant manner, but as he had sewn her up with black stitches, all beans since then have a black seam.

The Straw, the Coal, and the Bean
Old folktale

Gramp's Beanhole Beans

Back when most people in this region put in a garden, lots of folks raised beans of one kind or another. Beans were taken seriously and everyone had a favorite: pea beans, soldier beans, navy beans, or yellow eyes. One of the prettiest was the red and white speckled variety known as Jacob's Cattle. It must have been a handful of beans very much like those for which Jack in the Beanstalk traded the cow.

When the beans had formed in the pod toward the end of summer, the plants were pulled and piled in heaps, or stacked around a pole and left to dry. When they had dried enough to rattle in the pod, the vines were carried off the field and the beans threshed out on a large square of cloth. Some used a flail with a light swingle so as not to damage or scatter the beans. We simply pounded away with a flexible peeled pole cut in the woods. After they were threshed, we lifted off the stems and pods and put the beans in a washtub, chaff and all. We waited for a good breeze, and winnowed by pouring them, from a pail held chest high, into a tub on the ground. A bransack in the tub kept the beans from bouncing out and being lost.

During the 1930s Depression, cash was a pretty scarce item, and the barter system came back into fairly general use. A lot of farmers raised beans and paid part of their store bill with them. In their turn, storekeepers used the beans to pay Dad when he was selling for Twin State Fruit. Dad, however, was expected to turn in hard cash to his company so he had to sell the beans wherever he could. He got quite a sideline going with beans and other things. Once he even took a yoke of oxen in trade for a storekeeper's bill, sold them, and made money on the deal.

Beans baked with maple syrup or molasses and served piping hot with Johnnycake smothered in butter, and beans cooked with corn as succotash have always been traditional foods in northern New England. Different families have their favorite receipts and methods of preparing beans but none was better than my grandfather's beanhole beans. Gramp learned how to make them either side of 1905 when he was on the Connecticut River log drives. When the drives ended in 1915 and he went back to farming year round, he quite often cooked up a batch of beans for family occasions or a church social. He used a river drive bean kettle he picked up in West Stewartstown, New Hampshire.

When Gramp cooked beans he and Uncle Bill, and maybe some of my other uncles if they were around, dug a large hole three or four feet deep in the sandpit up back of the barn. On the bottom they laid down a thick layer of football-sized stones and started a fire of four-foot cordwood, which was kept burning until the stones came to a soaking red heat. Raking the hot coals aside, they lowered the kettleful of beans, maple syrup, and salt pork onto the baking stones, using chains hooked to the handles. Gramp put a heavy piece of canvas over the lid to keep out dirt, and they filled in the hole, leaving the beans to cook overnight.

Saturday afternoon Gramp set up a tripod over the hole with a pulley block fastened to its top. The men dug down to the kettle, chained it to the pulley, and hauled it above the lip of the hole. After two or three stout planks had been shoved underneath, the beans were lowered onto them and pulled across to solid ground. With a long-handled quart ladle Gramp dipped the steaming beans into a couple of good-sized pots and we carried them down for supper.

Gramp cooked mostly yellow eyes and pea beans. Soldier beans were somewhat scarce in those days and only came into widespread use later on. But no matter what kind they were, when word got around that he had a kettle of beanhole beans neighbors and other folks showed up to buy a quart or two. There are still a few people left who think fondly on those beans. Anyone who ever tasted them knows there is nothing around today that can touch them.

As far as I know, the secret of Gramp's baked beans went to the grave with him. Here, however, is an old family receipt that my wife has used for many years. The maple syrup in it gives the beans a wonderful delicate flavor. Grade B syrup tastes better and is less expensive than Fancy or Grade A. If maple syrup is hard to get, a half cup of molasses can be used in its place, but the beans won't be nearly as delicious.

4 cups yellow eye, soldier, or pea beans
1 small onion
1 tsp. salt
1 tsp. dry mustard
4 tbsp. brown sugar
1 cup boiling water
1 cup maple syrup
¼ lb. salt pork. Score and place on top of beans.

Soak beans overnight, then cook until skins split. Put them in the bean pot with the rest of the ingredients. Cook from six to eight hours. Keep water level with beans at all times. Take cover off about an hour before they are done. Oven temperature: 300 degrees.

Here stands a fist,
Who set it there?
A better man than you,
Touch him gin ye dare.

Mother Goose

Great-Granddad Waters

An old saw has it that to a southerner, a Yankee is anyone who lives north of the Mason-Dixon line. To those living north of the line, the Yankee is supposed to be a New Englander. Southern New Englanders—those in Rhode Island, Connecticut, and Massachusetts—think of Maine, New Hampshire, and Vermont as Yankeeland. From here the situation becomes more specific. To these North Country folk the real nickle-plated, brassbound article is a native Vermonter. Native Vermonters, however, hold that a genuine Yankee is a farmer who eats apple pie for breakfast.

In point of fact natives living in the region described in this book are generally regarded by other Americans as the quintessential Yankees. If proof is needed, it can be said to

85

lie in the plethora of traits they continue to share with the people of three and four generations ago.

The problem with all of this lies in the concept of Yankee as stereotype. While stereotypes may be a convenient way of looking at a people, they nevertheless erase the individual and eliminate the idiosyncratic. In accepting the stereotype of what Yankees are thought to be, we fail to gain a sense of what they are really like.

Although I never met any two east Vermonters or New Hampshire border folk I thought were chopped out using the same cookie cutter, most of them do share at least a few traits in common. One of the foremost of these is a strong sense of independence. For me this is epitomized by my great-grand-father Waters, whom I met two or three times when I was a small boy. My father knew him very well and had a fund of Gramp Waters stories that he shared with me.

"Your Uncle Rinx and I were the only grandchildren that ever really got along with your great-grandfather Leland Waters. He was staying with Dad and Mother then; your grandmother was his daughter. He was a pretty salty old gentleman. He had a white beard and your Aunt Virgie set it on fire once when she lit a cigarette for him and he always thought she did it on purpose. She did, too. But he took a great liking to Rinx and me; if we were going to a dance or anything, he'd go with us and he was seventy-five then.

"He walked everywhere he went. Well, when he was eighty he disappeared. Dad came down to where Rinx and I were staying in the boardinghouse and he says, 'He's gone and it's up to you boys to go and find him.'

"The old man used to have a farm way over in Lyman, across the river. I said to Rinx, 'That's where we'll find him, over there in Lyman somewhere.'

"Right over the mountain—Hunt's Mountain—is where we found him. It was a good thirty miles and five miles of that mountain is uphill. I don't mean just a general grade, I mean uphill! We went over there and one of his cronies says, 'Hell, yes, your grandfather's down to Sandy's.'

"We went down and, by God, Gramps was there. Said to him, 'You coming back home?'

" 'Nope,' he says, 'I've hired out and I'm going to stay right here.'

"Well, this Sandy was road commissioner for the town of Lyman. Back in those days it was all horses. They'd strike out in the morning with their teams and it would be dark before they got home. Take their dinner with them because they couldn't ride back and forth. Sandy lived out in the woods. Said he'd like to have Gramps stay there 'cause his wife was alone all day long and it made company for her. He had two cows and Gramps was milking them. And he took care of the chickens and a couple of hogs. Did the work around there and got in the wood. So everybody was happy and he stayed there till he died at eighty-eight.

"He had had the nicest wife—my grandmother Emma Williams. They were as different as night from day. She used to make butter when they had their little farm. She'd shape it by hand into round patties. Back in the woods there, they didn't have ice. They had a spring back up on the hill that Gramps piped down to their house and that water was like ice. And she used to keep the butter right in that water.

Put it into a cheese-cloth bag and stick it right under the spring."

"There was a man, name of Clark, in Lisbon. He was a big cattle dealer. He'd go round in late winter when farmers were short of hay and buy up the cattle they had to sell because they couldn't feed them. And up in beyond where Gramps lived was country I can't even describe to you because there's nothing at all like it around here now. It was all backwoods, hundreds of acres of it—no houses, no fences, just wild mountain and hill country.

"Clark used to drive all his cattle out in there, turn 'em loose, and then round them up in the fall. They'd be wild by then. Well, once a long time ago, there'd been farms up in that country. There'd been a road out through there, but it was pretty well gone by then. Clark would come up there in the spring, just as soon as the grass turned green, and drive his cattle up the road by Gramps' place and turn them into the wild place. Every spring when Clark went through was about the time Gramps had his garden planted and Clark would drive his cattle right through the garden.

"It was Gramps' land. Clark had a right-of-way through it by way of the old road. But he didn't try to keep his cattle in the road, he let them feed as they went along. Gramps finally got pretty sick of it. One year he'd planted a lot of buckwheat and it was up in good shape. You plant that in the fall. Clark came and drove his cattle straight through it—flattened it. Gramps told him he'd have to pay for it and Clark said he'd be damned if he would.

"Gramps was about sixty then and he used a heavy cane

he'd whittled down from a piece that grew up from a tree root. Even though Clark was a much younger and heavier man, Gramps took that cane and gave him a licking—knocked the hell out of him.

"Clark had him arrested and he had to go into court in Lisbon. So Gramps went out into the woods and cut a small tree. It was six- or seven-foot long and so crooked you could aim for that table there and hit over here somewheres. So they went into court.

"Clark's lawyer stood up and went into a big rigamarole about what Gramps had done to poor Clark.

"And Gramps had brought this crooked six- or seven-foot club into court with him.

"Clark's lawyer spotted the club and he says to the judge, 'That's the club he hit my client with, Your Honor.' Says to Clark, 'Is that the club he used to beat you?'

" 'The very one,' says Clark.

"The judge asked Gramps who his lawyer was and Gramps says, 'I haven't got one.'

"And Gramps says to the judge, 'Your Honor, would you just step down here for a minute? Take this club and see if you can hit me with it.'

"The judge came down, looked the club over, and picked it up. Tried to swing it a couple of times. Then he handed it back to Gramps and went back up to the bench and dismissed the case. He said there was simply no way a small old man like Gramps could have used that club to beat a big, strong man like Clark.

"Oh, yes, Gramps had an occasional brush with the law.

Dad told me the two of them were fishing once and they'd got a bransack full of pickerel—they had way over the limit. And the game warden caught them and arrested them. The game warden had a buckboard and he said, 'You two get in there. I'm taking you in to Lisbon.'

"Gramps said, 'It's going to be crowded up front there. I'll sit in the back. I don't mind.' Warden thought that was great, so Gramps set in back with the sack of fish.

"Gramps always had a jackknife in his pocket and you could shave with it, it was so sharp. While my father kept the game warden busy talking, Gramps took his knife, slit a hole in the bag, and started tossing the fish out into the bushes along the way.

"When they got down to Lisbon and started into court, the warden went round to the back to get the fish. All he had was an empty bransack. No evidence. He had to let them go. Gramps was a clever old cuss; took a lot to get around him."

A Thirteen-Year-Old Buys a Team

Although Dad made it through eighth grade, he'd been earning most of his own living since he was ten. Here is a story he told me about "working out" when he was young.

"This Joe Blair had a big farm next the river just above McIndoes. I was thirteen years old and I went up there for the spring vacation and worked for him. Used to have a month or six weeks in spring that they'd close the school right down and call it spring vacation. He had a big dairy herd and a lot of horses.

"He had to take a sudden trip one time and he came up about eleven o'clock one night and woke me. Said Phelps, the horse dealer, had some new horses in from the West and he wanted me to take the old team down and pick a new one and bring them home.

"And I said, 'I don't know anything about it.'

"All he said was, 'You go down. I have told Phelps to let you have any team you pick out.'

"Well, I was down there at six-thirty the next morning and they had sixty horses and I looked at each one at least three times. And Dave Gatley, he was a local character, started hollering and telling me what to get for a pair of horses. 'I don't know why they send a goddam kid down,' he said. 'He doesn't know anything about horses.'

"Phelps heard him and he said, 'I don't care if he wants to look at them ten times apiece, you keep showing them till he makes up his mind. You understand that he's only a young boy, and this man has got enough faith in his judgement about horses that he sent him down here to pick the team instead of coming himself.'

"I finally made up my mind. There was a pair of stripe-faced bays with two white feet. Clydesdales. Big rangy fellows but they were a nice team. And I said, 'I am going to take this team.'

"And this Dave Gatley said, 'Jesus Christ, that shows how much you know about horses on a farm around here, long-legged horses like that.'

" 'I'll take this team and you help me get the harnesses on them,' I said.

"Phelps come in and he said, 'Got them picked out?'

"I said, 'That one, that pair of rangy stripe-faced bays.'

" 'You made a damn good choice,' he says. 'That's as

good a team as there is in the barn.' And he says, 'I don't know whether you can handle that pair of horses or not.'

"I said, 'You help me get them hitched up to that pung sled and headed toward the farm, and don't you worry about it.'

"So he did, and Phelps said, 'Dave, you hitch up my driving horse. I'm going to follow along behind and see he's all right.'

"Well, we hitched them up and when they went out the sled brushed the gate on both sides, it was flopping so, and they were right in a dead run. I had two sharp corners to make and I bet that sled went sideways about twenty feet on each one. And then I had five miles straight up hill. I had a nice whip and I put it right to them.

"Phelps was trying to keep up. The first pitch I come to they was lagging, don't you think they weren't, so I stopped them. I hung on to the reins but I got right out and took hold of the bridles and talked to them. And Phelps come along and he seen I was resting them and breathing them and not going to hurt them any.

"He says, 'You know I'm on a fool's errand. I'm goin' to turn round and go home. You're all right.'

"And he told Joe, 'You know something? That kid picked out the best team of horses there was in the bunch.'

"But I'd already had a lot of experience with horses with Dad, you know."

Now come the men with hammer and maul,
  Chisel and auger and block-and-fall.
Sweat and strain and peg and drive,
  This is what made the barn alive.
Honest labor and honest sweat,
  This is what leaves it standing yet.
Through summer's sun and winter's cold,
  Memorial to the men of old.

The Barn
C. F. Moody

Gramp's Barn

At last the time came when my grandfather and grandmother had grown too old to keep the farm going. One or another of their sons might have gone in with them, but Gramp was too stubborn to have a tractor and modern equipment on the place and the boys knew they couldn't make a living with just horses and human sweat. Finally Gramp sold the stock, and the farm became a very quiet place.

The farmstead sat facing the road within a half mile of the Connecticut. A few fields behind, the corpulent bulk of Roy Mountain rose from the edge of the hill country, its stony pate afire with the last of the sun. As the light failed, a cold paring of moon rose at the world's edge. Its pale light glittered on the metal roofs of the farm buildings far below; the smaller ones huddled like ships at anchor, close in to the loom of the barn.

Some time after midnight Gramp stirred restlessly in his sleep. Waking, he listened for the muted sounds of a farm in the middle watches of the night, remembering at once he would hear nothing. On this farm for several months past there had been no stock save the big team of Belgians kept out of a strong remembrance of days when the family circle was yet intact and the farm a hive of activity.

Though he could not hear them the old man knew well enough there were small sounds aplenty within the fabric of the barn itself. He had spent the best part of a lifetime working in its beamed and chambered duskiness; nights when as a younger man he'd crept quietly out of the house to gather sacking with which to cover the field beans against a killing frost. Other nights too, during calving time or when the Indian corn lay gathered for husking.

And at evening chores in the long midwinter nights he and Indian Joe, pitching hay down from the mows in the dim radiance of a kerosene lantern, heard the rafters creak under the weight of the falling snow piling up on the roof. Then the barn became a self-contained world in which the hiss of sliding hay and the desultory stamping of the horses marked the passage of time. The drifting path outside was the only sign of continuity with the life of the house.

In the early days of summer, before the hay was cut, the sun pressed hard against the cladding of the deep hay mow at the east end. It threw the whole interior wall, with its medieval pattern of board and beam and wind brace, into purest black, a black that was made all the more intense by the light that glowed at each crack and knothole.

When in the gathering heat, the iron roof began to warm with a quickening rush of metallic soughing and creaking, Gramp always stopped to listen. The wash of sound made him feel that in some mysterious fashion the ancient structure was stiffening itself against the weight of the day.

After Gram and Gramp died, the old barn stood for many years, large and foursquare against the sky, its coat of red slowly fading to a dusty rosy hue. Then the barn scavengers came and killed it and sold the massive timbers and worn boards to a rich man downcountry to build into a trendy home.

Part Three

Workingmen

Oh the buzzing of the bees in the cigarette trees
  beside the soda fountains,
Near the lemonade springs where the bluebird sings
  in the Big Rock Candy Mountain.

There's a lake of beer we can jump right in
  and the handouts grow on bushes,
In the new-mown hay we can sleep all day
  and the bars they have free lunches.

The mail train stops and there ain't no cops
  and the folks are tenderhearted,
Where you don't change your socks and they never throw rocks
  and your hair is never parted.

The Big Rock Candy Mountain

The Empty House

Quite often we'd hear "The Big Rock Candy Mountain" playing on the radio and snatches of it being whistled or sung on the streets. A wistful song with a note of pathos, it was an expression of the yearning of millions of poor Americans for the promised land of milk and honey. Somehow, with the hard times and thousands of men on the hobo trail, it seemed more appropriate as the American anthem in those years than the "Star-Spangled Banner" or even "America the Beautiful." It fit the mood of the people better.

White River Junction wasn't quite as hard hit as some of the large population centers outside the state. As a major north-country railroad town and distribution center, it provided a good many jobs. Sandwiched between the Connecticut River and the freight yard in White River Junction was a place known locally as Railroad Row. It was filled with large warehouse businesses. To each ran a siding of railroad track along which freight cars were "spotted" for offloading into the battered, homely buildings.

The summer I turned twelve, and for several summers thereafter, I worked at one of these places, the Twin State Fruit Corporation, the large fruit and general produce plant where my father worked. I can say without reservation that I never worked harder in my life. We unloaded and piled away sacks of potatoes, crates and boxes of fruits and vegetables, candies, cheeses, olive oil, and cases and barrels of ale, beer, and wine. The work was heavy and done entirely by hand. I still recall the many ingenious ways of interlocking the bags and boxes as we stacked them in tight, high piles.

In the work force were men from southern Italy, one Syrian, and a few Anglos. They went by a variety of nicknames: "Duke," "Fat Pete," "Push-'em-up-Mike," "Jo Jo," "Banana Mike," "Pigeon," "Lolly," "Minnie," and "Big Boy," to name only a few. They were, beyond any doubt, the toughest, most colorful men I have ever worked with. I worked a good share of the time in a rather peculiar unit of the operation—a place called the "Empty House." All told I must have spent two or three years at hard labor there.

With the repeal of Prohibition in 1933, the liquor industry quickly got back into business. Actually, it had never closed down, only now it was legal again. When I began at Twin State Fruit in 1936, the day of the easy throwaway was still a long way off. People in Depression times were "savers";

they saved everything—string, cellophane, tinfoil off cigarette packs and candy bars, lumps of coal picked up along the tracks—everything!

One thing the breweries saved was the "empty." Customers brought their empty bottles back to the stores and got a refund of two, five, even ten cents a bottle. The storekeeper shoved the empties, all mixed up, into cases out back. The cases of empty ale and beer bottles, tonic bottles, and kegs were faithfully (and with much cursing on the part of truck drivers and their helpers) carried down stairs and fire escapes from second- and third-story bars. Other empties came out of the backrooms and dank cellars of grocery stores and restaurants. In short, empties were stored in any available space, no matter how awkward or inconvenient it might be to get to.

After pickup, the empties were delivered to the Empty House, a ramshackle building at the top of Railroad Row. Three of us manned the cavernous depths of the place. We spent a lot of evenings sitting outside on the loading dock, smoking and envying our buddies who were at the movies or off swimming somewhere, while we waited for the trucks. To pass the time we watched the train passengers picking their way overstreet to the hotel, amid the din and smoke of switching engines and yard crews making up the trains.

Meanwhile, the truck crews conducted urgent business along the road; what with girl friends, poker games, and other activities, the loads often didn't arrive until eight or nine o'clock. We had to work far into the night unloading, counting, and pricing out each load. In the morning, we sorted and piled them away, each brand in its own place, till we got a freight car or truck load to ship back to the brewery.

We stacked the heavy, steel-hooped oak barrels in a pyramid that reached high into the rafters. And we drew straws to see who'd break down this barrel mountain on loading days. The loser, gingerly approaching the ordered ranks, seized what he hoped was the "key" barrel, pulled hard, and ran like hell to get out from under the tumbling cascade of potential cripplers. For a long time afterward the rays of sunlight slanting through the cracks of the ancient structure were thick with dust motes raised in the flurry.

The brand names, redolent of the thirties, are almost all gone now. Blue Ribbon lingers on but where can one now ask a barkeep for a Trommers White Horse Ale, a Utica Club, a Krueger, or a Haffenreffer? Coca Cola had been around for years but Pepsi was just getting known. We had Moxie (the real stuff), Mission Orange, Chocolate Five-O, and Canada Dry cream soda—and other flavors you don't find much, if at all, anymore.

Sorting the bottles was a long, slow, frustrating task. Brewery and tonic company sales reps insisted on getting back their own bottles and no others; unfortunately, bottles came in a bewildering variety of colors, sizes, and special shapes. The morning's sorting seemed endless. It *was* endless! It was also dangerous. Sometimes as we bent over the cases, our hands moving in a blur of speed as we snatched and placed the bottles, one of us would encounter the razor-sharp spire of a bottle broken in transit, with results better left to the imagination than described.

One thing that made the heavy work bearable in the stifling heat and smell of stale beer inside the old warehouse was the fact that storekeepers were careless. They often left one, three, even a half-dozen full bottles of beer or tonic in a case. Even when the storekeepers were careful, the driver and his helper were sure to remove a few empties, replacing them with full bottles from the store's stock. This wasn't exactly dishonest; it was merely a slight tariff due for much unnecessary labor suffered by the men in carrying and stacking the heavy barrels and cases for the store.

So, one way and another, because even the truck crews had a limit to their alcoholic intake and sometimes didn't find all the full bottles anyway, we in the Empty House were in command of an inexhaustible supply of the best ales, beers, and tonics. A couple of drivers, whose routes were upcountry, used to bring us large greasy bags of pork scraps, the crispy pieces left after fat pork had been "tried out" for its lard. With a beer or tonic they were delicious.

With such riches to command, we were able to recognize the potential for a symbiotic relationship when we saw it, despite the fact that we were young and certainly wouldn't have understood what symbiotic meant.

It happened in this way. We didn't enjoy drinking warm ale or tonic and we knew the railroad station, just across the tracks from the Empty House, maintained a great chest of crushed ice for the use of the trains. We put out a few feelers and found out that the men responsible for replenishing the ice were, to a man, possessed of an intense thirst. We dragged several outmoded ice chests from their place of storage in a backroom, cleaned them up, and hid them in a cavity hollowed out behind a distant stack of discontinued beer cases.

Then began the great invisible persons ploy. In the sweltering heat of summer, we made two, even three, trips a day to the railroad ice chest. Each time, we carried back five-gallon buckets filled with chunks of lovely clear ice. Train passengers stared, seemingly puzzled by our activity, but the railroad men took no notice at all.

Later, as we worked away among the barrels and cases, like Sisyphus with his stone, railroad men—always one at a time—wandered in. Studiously avoiding anything more than a pleasant hello, they disappeared behind the stack. A muted snap as a cap came off, then a long-drawn, heartfelt "Ahhhhhh!" After a minute or two, a newly refreshed railroader drifted back to the station, his cap tipped jauntily back on his head, a contemplative look in his eye.

Some made several trips a day but we never ran out of goods. Nor did we ever run out of ice. And we never saw any difference in the measured routine of the railroad operation in the yard across the way. If the stationmaster noticed the increased consumption of ice, he perhaps also noted the increased cheerfulness and willingness of his yard crew and was a wise enough man not to disturb a delicate balance.

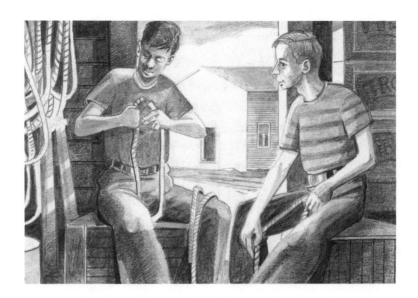

Banana Ropes

Twin State Fruit sold a lot of bananas. They were shipped green from Central America. We got them by the hundreds of bunches, packed standing on end, in freight cars. The day crew unloaded them, hanging the bunches from hooks in the ceilings of three special banana rooms. A few store owners liked to buy green bananas and let them ripen in their store windows as a way of drawing trade. But most grocers wanted nice yellow bananas ready or almost ready to eat. The trick for Twin State was to generate a steady supply of ripe ones for its customers.

As the bananas were unloaded they were separated by degree of greenness. The ripest were hung in the first room, the greenest in the second, and those in between went into

the third. The dead green ones were kept at a cool temperature to prevent them from ripening too soon. But the room
holding bunches with a touch of yellow in them was turned
into a kind of jungle to hasten ripening. The floor, strewn
with a layer of wood shavings, was wet down each day or so.
And three or four buckets of steaming water, sitting on gas
burners, fed a steady supply of warmth and moisture into the
air. As the bananas ripened they were sold and replaced by
green bunches from the other rooms. It took some doing, but
in this way it was possible to maintain the flow of ripe
bananas.

Well before the fruit arrived, we readied hundreds of
banana ropes, circles of rope that the unloaders carried in
bunches looped over their left arms. The men removed the
ropes one at a time, passed an end around the top of the
banana stalk, and pulled the other end through. With this
rope "handle" they dragged the bunches to the car door and
lowered them to the shoulder of a man standing below. He,
in turn, passed the bunches to men inside the building, who
carried them into the banana rooms where a man standing on
a box hung them from ceiling hooks. When the rooms were
filled there was barely room to walk between the hanging
bunches.

I hadn't worked there long when the boss sent my cousin
Charlie and me upstairs to get Ralph Littlefield to show us
how to tie banana ropes. Ralph was a debonair guy with a
cutting wit. (In another life he probably would have been a
playboy.) He'd already been a cowboy in this one and he
taught me how to roll wheat paper and Bull Durham ciga-

rettes with one hand. His work clothes were always clean and neatly pressed because he rarely got in on the bull labor. His domain was a fenced-off area that held the delicacies of the business: wines, olive oil, nuts, tinned specialty foods, and candy.

Ralph led us out between the stacks of beer and tonic to a cubbyhole beside the Trommers White Horse Ale. Taking a quart of Canada Dry cream soda from a half-empty case, he set it between a couple of overturned wooden boxes. Then he walked over to a reel of banana rope suspended in a two-by-four frame fastened to a post. The rope was made from two strands, one green, the other white, twisted together in a spiral. Fifty individual ropes, lightly bound together into a fat hawser, were wound onto the wooden reel. Ralph seized a banana knife sticking out of a crack in the post.

"Now listen!" he said. "You two may think tying the ends of a piece of rope together is a cinch. It's not, and there are three ways you can get in a lot of trouble. The first one is by not cutting the ropes long enough; that makes it tough for the men threading them onto the stalks and the men hanging the bunches."

He took a grip on the end of the fifty-strand coil of rope, and stripped some off the reel. Carefully wrapping it over his elbow, he brought it back to his hand, let go the end, and cut the coil in two just beyond his thumb. Then he did it again and handed one of the cut sections to each of us.

"Now," he said, "I don't want you boys measuring your rope the way I just did. Your arms aren't long enough. What I want you to do," he added, pulling out a piece from my

107

section, "is to use this rope right here as your measure." And he laid it on the floor beside the post.

"Got that? The next thing is don't tie the ends with anything but a square knot." He took a rope, tied the ends using the wrong knot, and gave it a sharp tug. The ends came apart.

"Now if that happens you're going to be sorry. I'm going to show you how to tie a square knot and then I'm going to watch you do it for awhile. This rope is slippery and any other kind of knot is going to work loose and drop the bananas on the floor.

"The last thing is be sure you make enough ropes. If the men run out in the middle of unloading they get pretty unhappy. So even though the job looks simple, and it is simple, you're going to do it exactly right."

"Yessir, Ralph," we breathed. He showed us how to tie the knot and give it a hard jerk to set it, then he threw the loop of rope over the bottle.

"Now," says he, "two thousand ropes ought to do it for this time. When you get done you can drink the tonic." He stayed and watched us for a while. Every now and then he'd pick up a rope and check the knot. Finally, satisfied we could handle the task, he went back to his own work.

It didn't take Charlie and me long to tie the two thousand ropes because we raced each other to see who was faster. In an hour's time we had bundles of banana ropes hanging from nails all over the wall. Then we drank the cream soda and went downstairs. We got our chance to see how good a job we'd done when the next load of bananas came in, and they put us in the car stringing the bunches and handing them down to the man feeding the line of carriers. One thing Ralph hadn't told us was that the rough rope, under the weight of the bananas, took the skin right off your hands.

That fall there was a docker's strike against the United Fruit Company in one of the Central American countries it treated as a banana-producing fiefdom. As a result, tons of bananas that hadn't been fumigated came into the States and some strange livestock came with them. It was cold enough when the next shipment came to Twin State that the creatures stayed in a dormant state during unloading. But when they hit the heat of the ripening room, things began crawling out of the bunches where they'd been hiding and they struck out for freedom.

Dad brought home some god-awful looking spiders and a big lizard that could walk upside down on the pane of glass, which was the top of his cage. A Dartmouth professor came and got them. He asked Dad to watch out for anything else that might show up. That Friday night something else did.

The night crew was putting up stock for the Saturday truck routes. A customer had ordered a bunch of green bananas which he wanted cut into hands to ripen in the store. (A hand of bananas is an individual cluster attached to the stalk.) Duke Scelza and another guy toted out an extra-large bunch and hung it on the scales. Duke took a banana knife and began cutting off the hands. He paused a minute and stepped back to fill his pipe. Just as he lit the match, a snake's head lunged from the bananas and struck at him. Duke and his helper yelled a warning and made for the safety of the office, the rest of the night crew tight on their heels. They slammed the door and locked it.

A brief discussion concerning what to do reached immediate consensus. It was best summed up by Fat Pete. "The hell with it," he said. "We ain't tackling that son-of-a-bitch with no stick or banana knife. Call the cops!"

A few minutes later a squad car drew up outside. Two officers, their shotguns loaded with buckshot, gingerly approached the snake's hideout while the night crew watched from the safety of the office. The snake was right there and ready for business. He came out after the cops and they blew him and the bunch of bananas to kingdom come.

I went to work that morning and found an excited crowd of customers and workers on the loading platform. They had laid the snake out for inspection. It was big. Someone said it was a fer-de-lance and poisonous as hell. I was happy to see it was deader than a doornail. Inside, what was left of the bunch of bananas still hung from the scale. The wall behind was splattered with buckshot and banana pulp.

"Just think," Duke said, "one of you guys on the day crew carried the bunch that had that bugger in it—right up against your ear."

*At last she saw a light in the distance. She went
towards the glow, and came at last to the top of a
mountain. A big fire was burning there, and round
the fire were twelve stones with twelve men sitting
on them. Three of them had snow-white beards,
three were not so old, and three were still younger.
The three youngest were the handsomest of them all.
They were not speaking but sitting silent. These
twelve men were the twelve months. Great January
sat highest of all; his hair and beard were as white
as snow, and in his hand he held a club.*

The Twelve Months, a Czech folktale

Cutting Ice

In November the land gathered itself and turned inward
against the cold. Ice crystals danced in the moon's glow as
nights lengthened. Each morning skim ice, edging ponds
and rivers, thickened and spread from the shore. Till the sun
got up the world was rimed in white, each weed stalk, twig,
and branch a delicate tracery of frost. Week by week Jack
Frost extended his domain over the hours.

Sometimes, skating in the long January nights, we saw the
northern lights. Far away beyond the Arctic Circle, shim-
mering curtains of green and red fire flickered eerily in the
sky. In the growing cold, ice thickened deep on ponds and
rivers. Now the harvest could begin.

H. P. Hood & Son, a Boston milk firm, owned a huge

icehouse beside the railroad tracks adjacent to the Connecticut River in McIndoes. They used ice in shipping milk and they also sent tons of it to the Boston market. My father told me how, at age fourteen, he worked with his father during the winter of 1918, cutting ice for H. P. Hood & Son. Later, when he worked at the paper mill in East Ryegate, the men picked up a few extra dollars cutting ice for the mill during their time off shift. One way and another, Dad had a lot of experience at the ice trade.

Cutting began whenever the ice was thick enough, usually at the end of an intense cold snap in January or early February. For ten, maybe twenty, days in a row the morning temperature would have registered twenty to thirty degrees below zero. At those temperatures it was a foregone conclusion that a day of ice cutting began with a good breakfast. That first day, when they came in from morning chores and milking, Gramp crumbled a slice of Dill's Best and filled his pipe while Dad and Indian Joe helped themselves to cups of hot coffee and sat chatting quietly while Gram cooked breakfast, which began with bowls of hot oatmeal. Bacon and eggs came next, followed by fried potatoes with salt pork in milk gravy to pour over them. Toast with homemade jam, scalding coffee, and pie filled up the corners.

"Come on, boys," urged Gramp, "it's going to be almighty cold out there on the ice. Eat up! You'll need all the fuel you can carry."

After breakfast they dressed for the ice. Along the river, at that time, there was a more or less standard cold-weather dress for outdoor work like logging and ice cutting. First

112

came long, heavy woolen underwear. Then thick woolen pants, likely as not a pair of Johnson's, a light shirt and a heavy wool one, a sweater, scarf, and mackinaw or blanket-lined frock, and woolen mittens inside a pair of leather outsiders. Hats had visors and pull-down earflaps, though some men wore the toque and a few hardy souls only a felt hat. Often a pair of bib overalls went over everything under the coat. Footgear was a couple pair of light woolen socks worn inside felt boots and rubber overshoes. Some men wore woolen stockings and high leather moccasins.

After thus fortifying themselves against the cold, Gramp got Pete out of his stall, put a work harness on him, and the three set off for the river. Looking down from the rise at the edge of the village, they saw dark figures of men moving about the ice, opening up the field for the day's work. The dull red of a blanket coat, the flash of a bright scarf, and the blue-painted sleds made colorful contrasts with the broad white expanse of ice. In the pale light of early morning the scene looked like a winter landscape by Brueghel.

A couple of horse-drawn bobsleds were already on the ice near the end of a loading channel. One of the teamsters smashed the night's skim of ice and stuck two spruce loading poles down into the water, hooking the upper ends to the back of his sled. Now he was ready to pull the cakes of ice up the poles and load his sled. Other workers drifted by twos and threes down the temporary road onto the ice. Some were itinerants and "floaters"—tramps and out-of-work men from the outside—anxious to turn a few dollars. Some of them were hard cases, not to be messed with. A knot of men

113

huddled at a fire of slabs on the shore where, at noontime, lunches would be thawed and coffee boiled.

The ice was twenty inches thick. The crew had been cutting for a few days and the field was well established. Today a new section was being opened. The foreman sent Gramp over to lay it out and begin scoring the cakes with an ice plow. The job called for a considerable degree of skill and a good eye. Gramp was an acknowledged master. He turned his horse over to a big itinerant whose job it was to snake long strings of floating ice cakes out of the water onto the conveyor carrying them into the icehouse.

Dad and Indian Joe picked up a couple of the heavy cross-handled ice saws and went to sawing ice nearby. As the morning wore on Indian Joe gave Dad a nudge and pointed. They saw Gramp walking over to the man working with Pete. Gramp said something to him and the man turned his back. Gramp walked away and began scoring blocks again.

"What's going on?" Dad asked.

"That guy's abusing Pete, "Gramp said. "I told him not to do it again or he'd be sorry."

Gramp was not a big man. He was, in fact, nowhere near the size of the itinerant. But he was strong and a good boxer. A few minutes later the man looked round sideways at him, grinned, and hit Pete a good lick across the rump. Gramp walked over, spun him around, and knocked him into the freezing, black water. Then he grabbed a pike pole, wound it into the heavy mackinaw, and dunked him a couple of times before dragging him back out onto the ice.

There was no fight left in him. Somebody helped him up

to the boardinghouse for a change of clothes and a drink. The rest of the time he was there he was a good deal more caring for the horses.

The Smith

Fifty years ago, when much of the back country of Vermont was still settled, a maze of narrow dirt roads wound through the hills. One day when Dad and I were out hunting we met a man living beside a grass-grown track in the mountains back of Waits River. His name was Dan John Morrison, and he was born August 15, 1892, near Scottstown, Ontario, an apprenticed blacksmith by trade. He was working at the forge mending a cant dog, and he showed us the trick of shaping the hook so it wouldn't skate off the log but would "grab" strongly. He and Dad got to talking about horses and logging, and Dan told us a story about a secret method he followed when shoeing horses who had to work on ice.

116

"Iron and steel. We worked all that stuff. There's a difference, you know. Iron now, say for a sled, for sled shoes, you know, iron is no good—it's sticky. You got to use steel. There's quite a trick in all that stuff. Now a few years ago when I worked a blacksmith shop down here to Lake Morey, along in the fall of the year, a bunch of loggers had to move a big team way off onto another job to get out a big woodpile for their camp. They wanted to know if I could shoe the horses. Put some shoes on and harden up the corks [horseshoe calks] so they'd last quite a while.

"They says, 'We got a lot of ice to contend with there, a lot of ice. It's quite a ways to bring 'em back here to your shop and we'd like them corks to last.'

" 'I can do it,' I said. 'But you got to give me a day to do the job in.' I said, 'I'll get your shoes all ready and,' I says, 'they won't look any different to you. But I guarantee that instead of growing dull, they'll be growing sharp.'

"They couldn't get over that. Says, 'Well, why don't you go ahead and do it.' They thought they'd try me out.

"I said, 'All right.'

"So I did. I went to work and I got some horse rake tines. Spring steel, you know. I made the shoes just the same as I would for a summer shoe. Then, I turned around and split the corks open, see. Heat them up. Spread 'em open with a cold chisel. And I made little wedges out of this spring steel. Cut 'em off and drove them down in there, right in those corks. Then I bring them up to a welding heat, and weld 'em, see.

117

Then when I got 'em all done, all welded in them corks, I draw'd 'em up sharp. But the outsides was ordinary steel. It was a little softer than the wedges. I had chilled steel inside and hard steel on the outside. So the hard steel outside, it would wear away, and the chilled steel inside kept coming right back up. They didn't see me do that little trick.

"Well, by God, they started in. Took the team. Said, 'Oh, those shoes ain't going to last.'

" 'Well,' I said, 'you go ahead anyway.'

"They were up there about a month. The fella driving the team told me, 'We had a lot of snow and ice come, you know. And what happened was those corks stayed sharp. They just wouldn't wear dull.'

"They don't know to this day what I done to make them corks stay sharp. But it took me a whole day to make up them eight shoes."

Come all you gallant shanty boys to listen while I sing,
  We've worked six months in winter's frost, we soon will take our fling.
The ice is black and rotten, the rollways piled high,
  So heave away at the peaveys, lads, while I do tell you why.
Break the rollways out, my boys, and make the sticks to slide,
  Sharpen your corks and grease your boots and start upon the drive.
A hundred miles of water ahead before you hit the town,
  So hang upon the tail of her and keep her running down.
When the drive comes down O, when the drive comes down,
  Each shanty lad in heaven would swap his golden crown.
Swap it all for a peavey stout, and an April pouring rain,
  And to birl a log beneath him as the drive comes down again.
When the drive comes down O, when the drive comes down,
  It's then we're paid our cash O, and then we own the town.
The streets they run with whisky, when the shanty boys so frisky,
  Set their boot corks in the sidewalks, when the river drive is down.

                                        Lumberjack's song

When the Drives Came Down

Not long after I had finished my boat, *Yankee Pine*, Gramp
drove down from McIndoes to see her. She was moored to a
thick iron ring forged through the eye of a heavy bolt driven
deep into the living stone of a ledge beside the river. Hammer marks from its forging still lay on its curve. The metal
had weathered to a rich dark brown pitted like the skin of an
orange—wrought iron put in a long time ago. When he saw
the ring Gramp said, "On the drives we used to boom logs
here. Gather 'em up 'fore we went on down the river. Boom
chains were short pieces of chain with a swing pin at each
end. We drove each pin into the end of a log and strung 'em
out across the river like a big fence. We chained one end to

this ring here and the other to a tree over there in Vermont."

I rowed him upriver to Lower Falls and he lit his pipe while he studied the torrent of water. When the tobacco was drawing well he told me what it was like taking the drive down through there.

"We carried our horses on rafts and when we hit the falls here we took 'em off and walked them around. But we ran the rafts right down through. Steered 'em with pike poles.

"There were bad places like this all along the river where men were drowned. One of the worst was down at Sumner's Falls a few miles below here. We had an awful time down in there. We lost a man once, right at the head of it. It runs on down and way out around in what we called a 'fiddler's elbow.' And there it drops over 'cause it's all stone ledge underneath. Van Dyke blasted a channel through there to run the logs in. And the waters *run*! I've seen one of those long logs, maybe sixty-five foot long, come down over that fall and I've seen it pitch up and then go straight down out of sight.

"Logs would wash up on the rocks and catch—start to make a jam. And we'd run in with a cant dog and give the log a snap and a twist and it would go flying. We had our accuracy. We knew how to handle logs."

When we rowed back down to the mooring he climbed out and fastened the boat to the ring. I passed the oars up to him and we sat on the sun-warmed stone a long time, smoking and talking.

When Gramp was young, men flocked to the North Country to cut timber in the big woods all winter and then come down with George Van Dyke's Connecticut Valley Lumber Company log drive in the spring. Dad just missed the drives but he saw them go through McIndoes and for the time the drive lingered there each spring he and the other boys never went to school.

"The drive used to set up about halfway between McIndoes and Barnet," Dad told me. "We'd be sitting in school and hear a shout, 'The drive's coming.' We'd run out the door and that's the last they'd see of us. They'd be there a month till they got through sweeping the rear. That was their headquarters. They used horses to pull all those logs that got washed out on the meadows back into the river.

"The year I was nine, Montgomery was running a store near the railroad underpass. McIndoes was dry and he used to get small kegs of Jamaica ginger sent up to him from Boston. It had a lot of alcohol in it. He asked me if I wanted to work for him doling it out to the men working the drive. So I sat in the backroom with a measure and the men'd come in and pay and I'd pour it out for them. Ten cents a drink. They'd down one or two shots and then head back to the camp. They were rough, strong fellows but they had a code.

"They were nobody to fool with, though," he continued with a grin. "You take your grandfather's brother, Charlie Hastings. He was on the drives, too. He was a small man, only one hundred twenty-five pounds, but he brought down a big hulk of a man working in Van Dyke's sawmill in McIndoes. Charlie was in there one day and the guy kept picking on him. When he wouldn't quit, Charlie turned a handspring and put both boots into his face. Took him right down flat.

121

Then he worked him over with the boot calks to take the gimp out of him."

Gramp said the Connecticut River log drives were the longest in the world and arguably the most perilous and difficult. There probably aren't more than a handful of people outside the region today who even know what a log drive was, let alone its sweep and grandeur. In the late 1800s and early 1900s, woods covered Vermont and New Hampshire from Wells River and Woodsville north into Canada. The Connecticut divided the two states and into it flowed tributaries with wild sounding names: the Ammonoosuc and the Wild Ammonoosuc Rivers, the Mohawk and the Nulhegan, Nash Stream, the Swift Diamond and Dead Diamond Rivers, Halls Stream, Indian Stream, and the Magalloway.

Logs were cut all winter long. Twitched out by horses and loaded onto sleds, they were stacked into towering piles on landings beside these northern streams and rivers whose waters had been impounded by an intricate series of dams. A whole range of dam types existed, some permanent, others expendable—meant to be blown—just at the time spring flooding was at its height along in April. Then the drive was on. The men drove millions of feet of logs down the tributary streams of the Connecticut into the main river. The drive went down the length of the Vermont–New Hampshire border into Massachusetts where it ended at Mount Tom in Holyoke.

The cowboy movie has left us an indelible picture of what a cattle drive was like. As a result, cowboys have become the quintessential American folk hero while the lumberjack has been forgotten. In some respects a log drive was quite similar to a cattle drive. Both dealt with herding a chaotic, moving mass of heavy objects over long distances. True, a steer is a living creature while a log is inanimate. But this was more than offset by the fact that the logs in a drive numbered in the hundreds of thousands, and as soon as they hit the waters of the river they melded into a confusion of twisting, bucking objects far bigger and more unpredictably deadly than cattle. The river driver was expected to work on this moving mass, jumping and running from one log to another without benefit of saddle and stirrups. Between him and a watery grave, there was only the precarious purchase afforded by his skill and the needle-sharp calks in his boots.

"River men," said Gramp, "were rugged, now I'm telling you! We were used to hard work and we got good pay for it. Back then, if you worked for a dollar and a half a day, well, that was attractive pay, you know. The drive was a hire from beginning to end. It was a follow game more than anything else."

Accidents in the woods and on the log landings killed a lot of men. And a lot more drowned in chutes and rapids. Their mates buried them on the riverbanks—their calked boots nailed to a nearby tree for a gravemarker. The icy waters of the Connecticut and its network of tributaries up in the North Country were as dangerous as hell and nothing to fool with.

Bridges, ledges, and sandbars caught the logs, many of which were giants sixty and more feet long and more than three feet through on the butt, piling them up by the millions of feet in logjams more complex than the Gordian knot. If they couldn't be picked apart with cant dogs, they were blown with dynamite. This was one place a bateau came in handy.

"We'd tape our dynamite to the ends of long poles," Gramp said, tamping a new load into his pipe. "They were handled by a man perched in the stern. Four men rowing backward took him into the face of the jam to a spot where the dynamite would do the most good. He jumped out onto the jam and they held the boat steady while he stuck the dynamite down into the logs and lit the fuses. Then he jumped back in and we scrambled out going hell-for-breakfast, straining at the oars to get out before it blew."

On the drive, bateaux were used as a kind of pack horse in freighting boom chains, bedrolls, supplies, and tools. They lugged hot meals from the *Mary Ann* (a cookhouse built on a raft) to the men out on the logs and along the shore. Men were ferried in the bateaux to the spots they were most needed. One bateau carried an anvil and portable forge for the drive blacksmith to use to repair broken equipment and to shoe the horses.

Dad told me Van Dyke moored a slew of bateaux in the Connecticut at McIndoes and the village boys used to play in them.

"They were a big boat. A dozen men, or more, could ride in one. They were made mostly of spruce. It was a tough wood and could stand a lot of knocks. The men usually rowed them standing up. They had seats but they were loose so they could be shifted. There was a small seat in the stern where the steersman sat and he steered with a big paddle. I remember they had light racks in the bottoms, between the ribs, to protect the planking from the calks in the men's boots."

Gramp described bateaux this way. "They were much bigger than your little boat there. They were a big boat that was pointed on both ends. They'd run anywhere from twenty-four to thirty-three feet long. They were peaked up in the front and they laid open farther back in the belly part. That peak was made like that to spread the waves, 'cause we run 'em right over the falls. We built them all of wood and they were rugged. We most always pushed 'em with poles, what we called a pike pole. It was a long pole with an iron brad on the end.

"We painted them a dark blue that was almost a purple. Generally there'd be four to six men that would run the bateaux down through the falls. It was a heavy-duty boat. I've seen twenty men in one. It would sink the boat down quite a little bit. But boy! Any ordinary river water they could handle. We always carried oars in the boat, and if the water was deep we'd row instead of poling 'em.

"We pitched the bateaux every spring before the drive. Used pine pitch and lard mixed together and heated. We'd turn the boat over and burn the old coat off with a red-hot pitching iron. That was a wide piece of half-inch iron with a rod welded onto it for a handle. And the handle had a jog in it, so's it'd keep your hands up away from that hot pitch. Then we put the new pitch on. You'd follow the seams so the heat would melt the pitch right down into 'em.

"On the drive there'd always be some men working while

the others were eating and sleeping. We had shifts and a mealtime schedule. They fed us four times a day and we had a midnight supper, too. We slept in big tents. They had blankets for us. They had places to wash and keep our things clean. We rolled our blankets and tied them when we weren't using them. The bedrolls had our name on them. They were carried downriver in the bateaux, and other stuff went on the rafts.

"We had kerosene torches for light. Hung them on the trees. All our equipment was topnotch. It was a profitable business for Van Dyke. There was always a bunch of boys hanging around and once Van Dyke, he said to one of them, 'Get me a pail of water.' And the boy got the water quick and he got a five-dollar bill put in his hand. The boys loved the drive. Course we wouldn't let them anywhere it was dangerous. It was quite a show to see. We had about everything you could think of in there on the tail end. Ten or twelve of those big teams, cant dogs, pike poles, boats and rafts, and all the men.

"Now cooking on the drive was interesting. The cook had to be a cook—I mean an old-fashioned cook. He had to know his business. He made cookies of all kinds, cakes and bread and everything you could think of. His cake was as light as a feather and it was frosted, too. Different kinds of cake so the men had a choice. They'd go right in and help themselves; there it was, all in rows. They cooked lots of pea beans and yellow eyes. Put in plenty of salt pork and molasses. One of the big things was baked beans cooked in the ground—nicest baked beans you ever saw. Those bean kettles were made

126

with a steam channel cast right into one side so they wouldn't boil over.

"Served it all up on tin plates. Then we had bread and tea and Boston coffee. Had a great big tin coffeepot. It was big at the bottom and it tapered up to the top. It hung in a cradle so all you had to do was just tip it. Made fresh and it was there all the time. Everything was clean. They rolled out fresh white paper on top of the table for each meal."

Gramp knocked the dottle from his pipe and got up and stretched. "Well," he said, "that's all over now. I wished they'd lasted long enough for you to see them. They were exciting times."

Gramp and the Bootleggers

Gramp had little use for Washington and held politicians in low esteem, viewing them as dunderheads at best. His opinion of them at their worst can hardly be set to paper. And during the late twenties Gramp held strongly that Prohibition was a mighty token of the bunch down in Washington at their dead level worst. His sympathies lay with the bootleggers with which this region fairly teemed. In this he was no different than a great many other Vermonters.

These sentiments got a mighty jolt the day the bootleggers killed his favorite cow, Daisy. Gramp and Indian Joe were driving the herd back from pasture one afternoon during corn harvest time. They were driving the cattle along the edge of the road till they could turn them up the back lane to the barn.

Two bootleggers, driving a Cadillac touring sedan at a high rate of speed, hit Daisy, the best Jersey milch cow in the herd. A cow is a pretty solid object! The big car caromed off the dying Daisy and, still going fast, hit the old maple at the edge of the lawn, dead center.

There was a shriek of tortured metal and a shattering of glass. The two bootleggers crawled from the twisted remnants of the Cadillac and hit the ground running. It wasn't a fast run, more a kind of limping jog because they were pretty well battered. But it was fast enough for them to make their escape from Gramp and Indian Joe who had Daisy and the rest of the herd to contend with.

Gramp was enraged! After the herd was in the barn he got a thick logging chain, rove it in and out through the now exposed structural detail of the car and padlocked it to the tree. Then he and Joe examined the wreckage thoroughly. The first thing they found was a wooden case of premium Scotch whisky. Gramp set it carefully to one side, well out of sight. Then he struck pay dirt under the hood. He found a curiously wrought Rube Goldberglike device known in the liquor trade as a "smoker." Gramp knew he had the bootleggers. The smoker would be a dead giveaway to the sheriff that he'd got hold of a car used to run liquor down-country.

After milking and chores that night, Gramp and Indian Joe got a lantern and some tools and removed the smoker from the car. Bootleggers hated to lose a smoker. If hard pressed by the blockaders, a driver carrying a load of liquor pulled a cable fixed under the dash, releasing a thin stream of raw oil

129

onto the red-hot manifold. This produced a thick impenetrable smoke cloud under cover of which the driver often made his escape. Indian Joe was even stronger than Gramp. He carried the thing up the side of the silo, dropped it in, and the next day they put it under ten feet of corn silage.

In a few days, when they thought Gramp might have cooled off, the bootleggers sent a couple of emissaries with enough money in their pockets to pay double the cost of Daisy. As an opening step in his side of the negotiations, and also I suspect as a matter of conscience, Gramp threw them bodily off the farm with a warning not to come back. Now it should be understood that the liquor trade in this region was more of a sporting proposition than elsewhere. All sorts of people were involved. Certainly they were serious about the profits to be made. But the people in these hills carried, as part of their cultural baggage from the British Isles, a tradition of making and using strong drink. Its occasional use was an ingrained part of their lives. The risks they ran in flouting a thoroughly unpopular law were part of the fun. There was, for example, a kind of unwritten gentlemen's agreement that Federals and bootleggers would not shoot at one another. Through occasional excessive enthusiasm on one side or the other this did sometimes happen, but at least the gunmen were careful to try not to hit anyone.

So when Gramp proved adamant in his refusal to surrender the smoker, all that happened was that several more courteous overtures were made, upping the ante each time. Still Gramp would have none of it. Finally the chief of the operation, a respected pillar of the church in a not-too-distant town, sent word to Gramp's sons.

"We've been nice up to now," he said, "but I am beginning to find your father a little unresponsive. Why don't you boys come out to the house and talk with me." So they went. The place proved to be more of a mansion than a house. They were admitted by a maidservant. Good cigars and strong drink were proferred and accepted. No threats were made but their genial host left them with the impression that if Gramp couldn't bring himself to accept the latest generous offer and give back the smoker, he might well find himself up against a set of odds that he and the boys couldn't possibly deal with. Gramp intended to surrender the smoker eventually; he was only waiting till the price was right. That night he knew it had gone as high as it was going and he gave in.

Next morning a heavy black automobile drove into the dooryard of the farm. Two men in expensive suits got out and shook Gramp's hand. After the money passed, one said, "All right now, where's the smoker?"

"Come with me," Gramp grunted and led them into the barn. He grabbed two silage forks. "Follow me," he commanded and climbed up into the top of the silo. Pointing to the corn, he said, "Dig!"

Two hours, and two ruined suits later, the weary men departed the farm with the smoker. Gramp had given them a couple of drinks of their own Scotch to encourage them. They were cheerful enough to acknowledge the joke.

Later that year, after the snow had come, Gramp and my uncles talked about the incident in the dining room one night after supper. Gramp had the last bottle of the bootlegger's Scotch on the floor by his chair. From time to time he poured a tot all round. The old man gagged a little as he knocked it back. Dad asked, "What's the matter Gramp, don't you like good Scotch whisky?"

"Course I do," Gramp replied, "but, by God, boys, I thought I'd never get down to this last bottle. Indian Joe's drunk the most of it. Every time I go to take a drink of the damn stuff I think of Daisy and I get so mad I can hardly get it past my nose!"

Heap high your golden harvest,
Heap high the golden corn.
No richer gift hath Autumn bestowed,
From out her golden horn.

Anonymous

The Ewie wi' the Crookit Horn*

One of my favorite uncles had a big touring car equipped with a smoker and an oiler. With it he ran many loads of booze over the border from Canada. And as a kid I worked with a bunch of men who, just before Prohibition ended, loaded a car with weapons and sallied north one night to highjack a truckload of liquor coming down from Canada. They got away with it, too.

Among my friends is George Fordyce Ritchie who taught me to play the bagpipe many years ago. I knew he'd been mixed up with bootlegging but he was pretty close-mouthed

---

*The name of an old Scottish strathspey. Contrary to what one might think, "The Ewie wi' the Crookit Horn" was not a female sheep with one horn crooked. The "ewie" was a Scotch whisky still and the "crookit horn" was the twisted worm from which the whisky dripped.

about it. Until one day when I asked him, and he suddenly began to tell me what it was like.

"It was a completely different world then than it is today. Like we were bootleggers and everybody in town knew it. But, boy, you were on the top of the heap. Better than being the president. And if you wanted a little cooperation from anybody, they'd do anything for a bootlegger, even if they never bought nor drank any booze. You didn't have to be afraid of the public.

"You take when we were getting a load out. We'd have assistance to find out where the blockade or the revenue was. We had a man to ride 'pilot' for the load. To scout ahead and locate the blockade you know.

"I had bought an old 1910 or 1912 Indian motorcycle. It was a big one with a carbide headlight on it, had to light it with a match. One of the bootleggers says to me one day, 'George, didn't I see you riding a motorcycle the other day?'

"I said, 'Yeah,' and he said, 'How would you like a job?'

"I says, 'Doing what?'

" 'Riding pilot,' he answers.

"Well, I tried it but the roads were all sand and pretty rough and after I'd flopped a few times I started driving pilot in a car.

"Way it worked was the pilot car went first. It come down two or three miles ahead of the load. If there was blockaders they'd stop you, of course. Search your car and everything. Say, 'O.K. Fine. You may go.' So we'd turn right around and head back and stop the load, say, 'Watch it! They're down at such and such a spot.'

"So the load turns and goes back. But we had other ways, too. We'd go down the road so far and into a farmhouse. We knew all the farmers along down through. And the load would be hid out at a farm, say five miles back. And we'd call them. In them days the telephone operators could hear everything. So we had a code, you know. He'd say, 'Have you got any hay to sell down there?'

"And I'd say, 'Yes, we have,' or 'No, we haven't.'

"We'd talk a deal but the words he was listening for was the 'yes' or 'no.' 'Yes, we have' meant 'Yes, come on down, you're in the clear.' But if I said, 'No, no, I'm short of hay (or wood or whatever), I'm afraid I can't help you,' it meant 'There's a blockade set up on the road. Stay where you are.'

"So you'd give these farmers a couple bottles of booze or a dollar and down the road you'd go. But the point is that today people would think, 'He ought to be in jail,' and they'd turn you in. They were all heroes in them days. Different world now.

"Course there were times we'd get caught carrying a load. Like they'd block the road with a car. Supposedly you couldn't get by, but we'd make a stab at it sometimes. You might lose the side of the car but if you didn't blow a tire you could get away from them. We had good cars, Cadillacs and Packards and all that. But you might lose your car and the load, just have to leave it and get out and run for it.

"Just once they shot at us. Old Joe Parsons, he was probably the best driver of the whole lot in them days. He was about six-foot-three, and if he hadn't been so bowlegged he'd have been seven-foot tall. The revenuers shot at the tires of a car they were chasing in New Hampshire and the guy went into a stone wall and got killed right there. Well, we were night birds, you know, but we used to talk to the revenue officers in the daytime—go and visit them. They knew what we were doing just as well as we knew what they were doing. So after that shooting happened we got talking about it with them. All friendly 'cause we knew it was their job and they were just collecting a week's pay. We used to tell them, 'If it wasn't for the bootleggers you guys wouldn't be working.'

"So, anyway, they brought up about the revenue shooting the tires off that bootlegger's car, and him getting killed. And Joe P. told them right then and there, he says, 'Now look! We've had a lot of fun up here. We've enjoyed our-selves real good, and we've always done it in a friendly manner. But nobody ever wants to point a gun at Joe Parsons or any car he's in. They better do a good job the first time or I'll come back with a gun and it'll be a two-way war. I mean it!'

"And they knew it and that ended it right there. They'd do this, though. Drive spikes through a plank and throw it down in the road to blow your tires. Things like that, you know.

"I never got caught. The nearest I ever came to it was with Dresell Coffin one night. We had a Packard and we came down the road and for some reason or another the pilot car was behind us. We were in front with the load. Well, they had a blockade in the road and Dresell, he pulled over into a farm and tried to turn around to run for it. He got his wheels onto a steep patch of grass and the car just sat there and spun. So he set the brake, opened his door, and he was away into the fields. I jumped out into the farmyard and I heard footsteps running, they was right there. So I ran in onto the barn floor and I see there was no place to go. There was two of them had come right in behind me and I got away from both of them. I just turned around, got down low, and went between them just like a scared rabbit. I crossed the road, went over a fence, and waded a river into a woods. Closest call I ever had.

"I'll tell you, those bootleggers were smart. One night they came down with a load and they had to run a roadblock. They lost their fenders, running boards and one thing and another. But they got away and around five A.M. they came through Montpelier headed for Barre. The law had phoned the Montpelier police and told them to be on the watch for a car with one side pretty well ripped away. So they were driving along and the car quit. The driver went somewhere to phone for help because the thing was sitting there loaded with liquor. They always ran two men to a car, and all at once the cops pulled up and arrested the second guy. He says, 'What are you arresting me for?'

"And the cops said, 'Whaddaya mean? You're sitting here in a car full of booze.'

"So the guy says, 'Oh, is that what's in those cases? I don't know anything about that. I was hitchhiking about a quarter mile back and this car came along and gave me a ride. Then it broke down and the driver's gone to get a tow or something. I don't even know who he is.'

137

"When the driver started back he saw the activity around the car and backed off. Later on, the guy that owned the car and the load came down where it broke down and went over the lay of the land. Over across the river was a farmhouse and he went over there and talked to the farmer.

"He says, 'Right over on that road there, I had a car with a load and it broke down and the cops got one of the men in it. He's going to have a trial at such and such a time. Now it's quite possible you came out of your house early that morning to go to the barn to do chores just about then. And it's possible you looked and saw that car stop to pick up a hitchhiker, then come along a little ways and stop. And then you saw a man leave the car and walk off.'

"When it came to court that's the way the farmer testified and they had to let the man go. Prob'ly slipped the farmer a hundred dollars but, like I say, there's a million ways. Most of the ordinary folks was on the side of the bootleggers.

"The revenue collected the cars when the bootleggers jumped and ran. They'd get so many and auction 'em off. The bootleggers'd go down and buy their own cars back for twenty-five bucks. I ran pilot from Canada with those fellows for about a year. Then I had a still up in Orange for three years.

"It was in a hunting camp up there. No way to drive in to it. We used to walk up the mountain better than two miles, carrying the stuff in on our backs. A hundred of sugar and a hundred of malt. It took that and a hundred gallons of water to make a batch of moonshine. We'd take that sugar and simple syrup it on the stove. Boil the water and just keep stirring in the sugar till it dissolved, then pour it into the barrels. Put fifty pounds of it in one barrel and the same in the other. Then just take and put one-half bag of mash into each barrel. Stir it up and let 'em sit. Depends on the weather. Sometimes in cold weather it would take more than two weeks for it to work. In good weather it would work in less than a week. While it works, all the mash floats to the top, then when it sinks to the bottom it was all set. Ready to distill.

"I made the still. 'Twas a copper wash boiler, a big one. Soldered the top on. Cut a round hole in it, with a brass clean-out cover so you could pour the liquid from the mash in. The coil, or worm, came out of that cover and then went round and round through a bucket and out the bottom, so's water could run 'round it to cool the distillate. I had a draw-off on the bottom of the pail.

"We set the wash boiler right on the stove over a hot fire. The mash turned to steam and went out through the worm and the cold water surrounding it condensed it to alcohol. The first that came through was ninety-three percent which is about as strong as you can make—can't make one hundred percent pure alcohol. We used a hydrometer to test it. When it began coming out of the worm at sixty-five percent we dumped out what was in the boiler and filled her up with some more out of the barrel. A lot of people would have kept right on till it was probably fifteen percent alcohol. We were kinda foolish because the people we sold it to used to add three to four parts of water to it and we could have run it down to below, say forty-five percent if we'd wanted to. Be that many gallons ahead, but we didn't.

"We strained it through charcoal and sold it for twenty-four dollars a gallon. Sold it to people—to farmers. We'd go through every two weeks, or as long as it took us to distill another batch. Some people took one gallon, some took two. We used to make two hundred and twenty-five dollars off of each batch. In other words we used to invest twelve dollars and get around two and a quarter in return. We spent it just as fast as we got it. I learned how to make moonshine from a guy in Chelsea. One night after a dance I went with him where he'd built a shack in the woods by a brook and helped him run a batch off. That's all I knew about it and it was all I needed to know. After you see it once, that's all you need.

"We took turns carrying the shine out in a packbasket. The keg just fit down inside so you couldn't see it. The very last time we came down out of there with a keg we almost got caught. I was carrying the basket on my back and we'd got almost down to the road when we met Zeke Dovere, the game warden. He looked at us kind of strange and he says, 'What in hell are you two guys doing out here?'

"Well, my buddy was pretty quick and he pipes up, 'Oh, we've been combing the mountain looking for whettlebark but we haven't found a bit.'

"Zeke stayed and talked awhile and that keg got heavier and heavier till I thought I'd sink into the ground with it. When he finally left we got out of there mighty quick.

"Every once in a while the sheriff, he got smart to what was going on and he'd lay for us. He had a Buick and I had an Essex Coach and he'd chase me. And I'd always just go down the road and turn right and go up onto the East Hill— just a narrow dirt road so steep that when they'd fresh gravel

the road you could get stuck just like you would in snow—
the wheels couldn't get a hold. But I'd go up there and turn
back down the hill to the village and he couldn't pass on that
dirt road. I'd go down the hill so fast that by the time he got
down there he wouldn't know where I'd gone. The road was
full of water bars and I'd have all four wheels right in the air.

"When we first started we put it up in little half-pint
bottles and took it to dances, but we took an awful chance on
getting caught. I was at a dance one night in Chelsea and I
heard a commotion out in the street. I walked out onto the
porch and looked down into the road, and here's my brother
standing out there beside his brand-new Maxwell talking to
Tom Dearborn, the cop. The cop had a bottle in his hand and
I say, 'Oh, oh, it looks like he's picked up my brother.'

"So I went down and elbowed my way through the crowd
right up in front of the cop and I says, 'Well, Tom what do
you know about that. I suppose you think you've got something there. Let me show you something.'

"I reached over and took the bottle out of his hand. I says,
'This is nothing but Coke.' And the minute he let go of it I
threw it over the livery stable down onto the ledges of the
brook. That's all there was to it. He had no evidence. He was
pretty mad but he had nothing on anybody.

"Tom was a problem. After us all the time. I was at a
dance over in Vershire with my pal, Archie MacNaughton.
Second floor and the stairs were awful steep, just like a
ladder almost. Archie was standing right there in the doorway and he heard footsteps coming up. He turned around
and it was Tom, the sheriff. Archie just reached up and

141

grabbed ahold of the top of the door jamb and let him have both feet right in the chest. He went down turning backward somersaults, you know, clear to the bottom. Archie got arrested that time.

"The bigtime bootleggers used to come to town. I've played billiards with Jack 'Legs' Diamond and Mad Dog Coll right in Barre when they were up there buying booze. Barre was a focal point of the trade. Barre bootleggers knew all the old dirt backroads over the Canadian border. So we would bring it to Barre and people from Connecticut, or Boston, New York, and New Jersey would come up and they would take it to their neck of the woods, you see. Or sometimes we delivered it down there, wherever it was going.

"One night we come down through and the revenuers had the road blocked. So we jumped and ran and the revenue officers took the car. And the first thing they done was turn right around and go back to their headquarters with it. So we come back in off the field and it wasn't long before our pilot car come along. We got into the car and Joe Parsons says, 'Well, let's get this thing turned around and head back.'

" 'What are you going back for?' they says.

" 'Oh,' says Joe, 'we're going back for the load. You want to know what they're going to do? They're going to drive right up to their headquarters, get out of the car, and go in and sit around and gas about how they got it and make out their reports and all that stuff. They'll leave the key right in the car.'

"So back we go. There's the car. Opened the door and looked in. There's the key. Joe stepped in, started it, and away we went.

"There weren't a lot of guys running stills up here in those days. Just a few like me. But the biggest still that was ever in Vermont was in Worcester, up above Montpelier. They didn't call it a still, they called it a 'thumper.' Two fellows came up here from Kentucky and here's how they done it. They went round all the booze joints and they would say, 'We're bootleggers and we've come from Kentucky and we know how to make corn liquor.'

"They'd say, 'If we can sell a big load of alky up here we're going to come back, build a still, make the alky, then deliver it and scram. Would you be interested in a full barrel, just a fifty-two gallon barrel of alcohol?'

"They went all around Barre, Montpelier, and Burlington till they had orders for all the alcohol they could pile on a truck. Then they went round again and said, 'Look, we've got enough orders. Is the deal still on?'

" 'Yep, I'll stand by my order.'

"So then they built this thumper. Got this old farmhouse way back on an old dirt road out of Worcester. And they built a solid wooden vat, like a silo's built. Iron rods around it, you know, and they soaked it and got it waterproof. Then they built a steam coil inside it and the piping went out to two forty-gallon range boilers, standing side by side over a stone-walled pit. You know what a range boiler is. It's what they used to heat and store hot water in with the old wood or coal kitchen stoves. Five-foot long and fourteen inches diameter. Well, they could burn four-foot wood down in that stone pit, see.

"They'd get up this head of steam and they had this wooden cover they could bolt down tight onto the wooden vat.

143

Their coil ran out through a tube of cold running water. So they put all the malt and stuff in the big vat and scrammed. When it was ready they came back and distilled it. They loaded it into their truck, delivered it to all the places and— *zap!* they were gone. That was the end. Nobody ever saw them again. Go in, make it, get their money, and be gone. Go to some other little remote place and do it again. Their idea was if you kept at it in one place you were going to get caught.

"Friend of mine found out about the thumper. He knew I made the stuff and he wanted the two of us to go in and run a batch through it. So I said, 'All right, we'll go take a look.'

"Well, we were driving down this old road and I looked and said, 'Well, Harold, there's somebody with a gun. Must be hunting.'

"When the guy turned and saw us he dove straight into the bushes. We went along up to the house and we was looking at the still, the thumper, and the guy walked into the yard with his gun. Turned out this guy used to help the Kentucky boys with making their booze and he was kind of a hermit. Lived in the woods there. Kinda pleased him we might start it going again.

"When we got done we started down the road and Harold says, 'What are we going to do with this?'

"I says, 'Don't say we—forget me! No part of it whatever. You don't think I'd get tangled up with that nut with the gun, do you? Not me, buddy. He'd shoot somebody.'

"He'd probably've shot the first Fed that stuck his nose in there."

Cutting Cordwood

When we were juniors in high school, my chum Nelse was given a shiny, black Model A Ford touring sedan. He was working after school at Hathorn's Garage, and one day the owner brought him out back, pointed to the car, and said, "It's yours if you want it."

It had a canvas top that folded down and isinglass side curtains for cold weather use. We did a lot of hunting and fishing with that car. After the hurricane of 1938 I well recall standing on the rear bumpers, clinging to the spare tire for dear life, to furnish the extra traction we needed while bouncing up a logging road on our way to fish some pond in the outback. As winter approached Nelse said to me, "By God, Perfessor (he never called me anything else as long as he lived), with the car to get around in we can cut some cordwood this winter and pick up a little spare cash."

I went to a man over in Sharon to see if we could cut for him. He didn't need us but my request for work put him in mind of a story about his grandmother.

"When my grandmother was a little girl in the 1870s, the two-man crosscut saw hadn't come into use yet. Falling trees, bucking 'em up into logs, and cutting firewood was done with the axe and bucksaw. She told me once that the menfolks on the farm would drag the logs they'd cut out in the woods into the dooryard to cut them up for firewood. Used oxen to do it. They were good men with an axe. The chips they made, some of 'em, was as big across as a dinner plate. Gram would go out across the snow to where they was choppin' and fill her apron full of those big chips. Then she'd carry 'em into the kitchen and put 'em into the oven. When they was red-hot, she carried 'em back out in a bucket for the men to stand on to warm their feet. It was bitter cold and their footgear wan't the good kind we have today."

Nelse had better contacts in the country than I did, and he located a man with a big woodlot and a desire to convert some of it into cordwood. Cordwood, for anyone who doesn't know, is incipient firewood. It's made up of small trees, limbwood, and sections of larger trees split length-ways into smaller billets. Split or whole, it can't run much over four or five inches in cross section. It is all hardwoods: rock maple, yellow birch, ash, cherry, beech, ironwood, white birch (which, though it looks pretty and sells well to summer folks, is not really good firewood), and sometimes elm, red oak, and whatall. Every piece has to be cut four feet long. When stacked in a pile four feet high and eight feet long you have a cord measure of wood—hence the ancient name, cordwood.

We began cutting late that fall after partridge and squirrel season ended. Winter came with lots of snow. We were working Saturdays and Sundays. Early in the morning, before light, we'd load our tools and grub into the Model A and drive out to the mountain woodlot. We packed the stuff in half a mile or so on snowshoes. Our tools, borrowed from our fathers and grandfathers, were the traditional ones: axes, a splitting maul and iron wedges, two bucksaws, rope, a two-man crosscut saw, falling wedges, and a cant dog to wrestle the logs around.

My axe was considerably lighter than the one Nelse had. At first he laughed at it but he soon changed his tune. It was a Finnish axe my father had owned since he was a kid. He told me once how he got it.

"The fall I was fourteen," he said, "this was in 1918, I went to work for a big lumber concern in McIndoes. They'd come up from Manchester, New Hampshire. Got wind of this mountain up there that had hardly been touched. There's a lot of woods between Groton and North Ryegate—all out through there—that had any amount of old growth lumber. Some of the pine was two and a half feet on the stump. Anyway, the company brought in a bunch of Finnish choppers.

"Those Finns brought a different kind of axe with them. It

147

was a single-bitted axe and had a wide blade: with the handle it wan't but two foot long. The local men used a bigger axe. Head three-and-a-half to three-and-three-quarters pounds and a long stout handle. The Finns made their own axe handles. They split 'em out and shaved them down much thinner. Those handles had a whip to them.

"The Yankees had a laughing-fit first time they saw those little axes. But you know they couldn't begin to keep up with them. They could strike a deeper cut with those little hatchets than we could with the big Yankee axe. There was one Finn there, Otto. I don't know what his real name was, they always called him Otto. I used to go eat with him a lot over to their camp. He gave me one of those axes. Those fellows would buy them a dozen at a time. I took the axe home. Dad was looking at it one night and wanted to try it. You know, inside of a week every man was using those axes just as fast as they could buy them off the Finns."

When Nelse and I got into where we were cutting, we stowed our tools and lunch buckets in a lean-to we'd built. Then we set posts eight feet apart, notching in a couple of slanted supports for each, cleared the snow away between them with a snowshoe, and began work. We piled the four-foot sticks of wood between the posts and a cord built up pretty fast, we being young and limber. We worked together at felling the larger trees, one at each end of the crosscut saw. Once the tree was down, we limbed it out with an axe and cut it up into four-foot lengths with the two-man crosscut saw. We split these logs into quadrants and eighths with the maul, iron wedges, and foot-long wooden gluts. Limbwood and smaller trees we cut with the axe and bucksaw. The brush-wood we stacked in neat piles.

It was healthy, invigorating work in the sharp, clear cold of the woods. Cold as it was, and sometimes it was cold enough that an axe got brittle and chipped on its sharp edge, we'd be sweating heavily in less than an hour. Then it was peel down to a sweater or maybe just a light woolen shirt till it was time for dinner.

By then our food was frozen and we had to thaw it out over the fire. We carried it in old-fashioned, enamelware lunch buckets. In the bottom was a slip-out container that we filled with coffee at the house. In the space above were nested sandwiches, pie, and a chunk of cheese. The top had a place for a cup to twist onto it. It was as handy a rig as one could wish. In mid-morning and afternoon we melted snow and brewed sweet strong tea with a chip of wood thrown in to settle the leaves. It was a good source of quick energy.

After we'd been cutting a few days I said to Nelse, "You know, a dollar twenty-five a cord is pretty slim pay."

"Just what I've been thinking," he answered, "what say we work a little air into the piles."

Piling cordwood is a long refined art in these hills. You can, if you know how, pile two seemingly identical cords, but one will have a good deal more wood in it than the other. That day we piled our last cord so it looked dense as kale in an oatfield but there sure wasn't a cord in it.

I guess the man we were cutting for must have known boys, for the next Saturday when we got to the cutting site, there was our last cord of the Saturday before—newly piled.

It didn't come to a full cord by a long chalk. We filled it up carefully. All the rest of that winter we piled a tight cord. He never did say anything to us, but he worked hard to hide a grin when we picked up our pay that night.

"You boys are doin' a good job," he said. "How're you holdin' out?"

"Just fine, fine," Nelse mumbled, and out in the kitchen we heard his pretty daughter giggle.

"Well, that's good. Sit right down here and have some pie and coffee before you go. Anybody's worked as hard all day as you two needs some fillin' for their frames."

We were taken from the ore-bed and the mine,
We were melted in the furnace and the pit—
We were cast and wrought and hammered to design,
We were cut and filed and tooled and gauged to fit.

The Secret of the Machines
Rudyard Kipling

Night Shift

A pal of mine, named Eddie, once helped me get a job working at a machine shop fifteen miles from home. We bought rides from Slim, a fierce, little, wiry-headed man, who lived with a sad-faced wife and a press of kids in a shabby, gray tenement. Slim owned a battered black Packard and a drinking problem. Every day he picked us up at 5:30 P.M. on Main Street in West Lebanon. At six sharp we opened our tool boxes and took over from the day shift at the Cone Automatic Machine Company in Windsor, Vermont. Through the skylights, high up in the roof, we watched the night draw down. At midnight the machines quit for twenty minutes while we ate from lunch pails. Dawn had broken before we handed over to the day shift six hours later.

Through the days—and interminable nights—the place was a world unto itself, its code of conduct and work ethic based upon working cast iron, steel, and bronze to extremely close tolerances.

That first night on the job I followed Eddie through the gates into the frenetic activity and racket of the main assembly floor. We paused by a pod of great gray machines. Fat steel drills, held in chucks suspended from thick complex arms, took dead aim at precisely marked points on heavy iron castings bolted to slotted tables below. Men standing in a scatter of sawdust spun cranks, set dials, and positioned tools in the light of lamps hanging below a smoky haze afloat above the machinery. Everything seemed to be done on a giant scale; to my unfamiliar eyes the scene looked strange and a bit scary. Eddie laid his hand on a massive metallic flank and told me it was a radial arm drill. "My machine," he said. "I call it 'Old Froggie.' " I thought he seemed a tad nervous.

Neither Eddie nor I knew that he was then at the zenith of his career as a machinist. His job changed a couple of times over the ensuing months—disaster seemed to overtake him in the small hours. He was always vague about details but I think the complexity of his machine was just too much for him. I recall his first demotion had something to do with a series of misdrilled holes in an expensive casting. Afterward I found him, one night, disconsolately running a small hand-feed drill press: a miniscule thing in comparison with Old Froggie.

Something went wrong there, too. Eddie was transferred

152

to making babbit hammers; a heavy tool used throughout the shop in setting up work for machining operations. The babbit was melted in a crucible in a tiny foundry, then cast onto a short iron handle. One morning, after a night of pouring rain, I met my pal at the Packard looking like an Egyptian mummy. His face and arms were swathed in white bandages. Somehow rainwater had leaked into the crucible of molten metal, and Eddie was dead center in the ensuing explosion. The experience erased any desire he might have had to continue as a babbit hammer maker. After this, although he came to work each night, Eddie disappeared from his old haunts. I found him at last, smeared with grease, running a mechanical hacksaw in the cut-off room. Hard at work sawing off short lengths of square steel stock, he was a pitiable sight. Eventually he quit and the place knew him no more.

My ride didn't last much longer either. One night, coming to work partly pickled after a daylong domestic row, Slim crawled inside the big machine he was assembling for a catnap. The riggers hooked a crane to it and began to hoist the machine for a move on down the line. Under the foreman's startled gaze a porthole in the machine's base suddenly flew open. For an instant Slim's panic-stricken face peered out, then he leapt. He landed hard and rolled against the boss's boots. He was docked his night's pay and told to go sleep it off in his car.

Instead, Slim climbed onto the factory roof and finished a bottle. Then, still smarting from the tongue lashing, he crawled to an open skylight, drew a bead on his boss standing far below, and threw the bottle. He missed, but the explosion of glass gave the poor man a severe fright. When he stopped shaking, he ordered the plant security staff into action. Slim was captured in short order. I knew something was up when I saw four guards drag him struggling and cursing through the toolroom on the way up to the office.

The three of us who rode with him gathered at the Packard that morning when the shift was out, but he wasn't there. We felt sorry. Young as we were, we knew Slim and his family didn't have much of a chance. We waited awhile, but he didn't show up. We straggled up to Main Street and began hitchhiking home.

I was put to work in the toolroom, a self-contained shop making a variety of jigs, fixtures, and tool-holding devices for the automatic machinery fabricated in the rest of the factory. The work was precise and some very fine machinists worked there. The kindly, grizzled foreman, wearing a tie and open vest, inspected me over the tops of his glasses. I knew what he was thinking—"greenhorn." He sighed and led me to a row of battered benches huddled along an outside wall. At each sat a mechanic engaged in the tedious, precise work of handfitting and assembly. I was told I was to be a burr filer.

"This is Frenchy," said the foreman, indicating a man at the bench behind mine. "He's going to show you what to do. Just ask him if you have any questions."

Blue bib overalls adorned Frenchy's stout body. Over them he wore a clean gray machinist's apron with a 0" to 1" micrometer in the swing pocket on the chest. In another pocket were a snuff tin and a 6″ machinist's rule. Frenchy used the rule to both measure things and to pack a fresh charge of snuff into his bulging lower lip. The pervasive smell of cutting oil in the air made cigarettes taste bad. Smokers, and that included almost all of us back then, either took snuff or chewed. Lots of benches had a tin can spittoon tucked underneath.

Frenchy's little black eyes bored into me from under a dark green eyeshade, secured by a strap around his head.

"What's your name, kid?" he asked.

I told him. "O.K., let's get you started."

He led me to the tool crib where I was handed ten brass tool checks on a ring and a heavy mill file. These, with a ball-pein hammer and a steel hook with a T-handle at one end, proved to be all the tools I needed.

Grabbing the hook, Frenchy led the way to a line of milling machines. The face and hands of the man running the first one were black as a boot. I soon found out why. He was taking slabbing cuts off castings with a Lovejoy cutter, and machining cast iron is dirty work. The work grew more complex (and cleaner) the farther down the line one went. At the very end, a lean gent wearing pince-nez glasses, starched white shirt, and a black bow tie operated a high-tech Brown & Sharpe Universal miller. As long as I was there I never saw a smudge on that white shirt.

Frenchy stuck the hook in a hole in a steel pan of slabbed castings, and I dragged it over to my bench.

"O.K.," he said, "now watch."

Taking a casting, he clamped it in the vise. Along one

edge ran a thick, ragged burr left behind by the milling cutter. Frenchy beat it flat with the narrow edge of the file, then filed it off using the flat side.

"That's what you gotta do, boy. If it's too thick, knock it down with the hammer."

That was my introduction to work in the toolroom. Monotonous, simple, and mindless, the work had to be done by someone and that someone was the greenest man. It was an initiatory rite. The old-timers kept an eye out to see how you were doing. They'd often give a push in the right direction, and you could pick up a great deal just by watching and from chance conversations. I soon found a way to get the burr off the piece in the shortest possible time.

Frenchy leaned over the bench one night. "For Chrissake, boy, slow down. You're gonna run yourself right out of a job."

Eventually that's what happened. Promoted to the first milling machine in line, I began making burrs for someone else to file away. I got to know Joe Cannon with the white shirt and bow tie, and the one-armed shaper-man who was shop steward. I became aware of the life going on beneath the surface in that roomful of artisans.

An aisle away, at right angles to the line of milling machines, sat a squat planer. Not large, as planers go, it nevertheless weighed several tons. Harry, its shepherd, had ringlets of snow-white hair and bright blue eyes. He spent his nights carrying out a series of exacting operations on castings so heavy they had to be hoisted onto the machine with a set of chainfalls. I did not then realize, but soon found out, that the chainfalls were capable of lifting a lot more than the work castings.

One night the sliding table carrying the work back and forth beneath the toolbit slid clear off the end of the planer. It thudded to the floor with a bone-jarring crunch. The foreman called a crew of millwrights and they hooked the chainfalls to the fallen soldier, laid it back in the ways, and it was soon going back and forth again. Harry had forgotten to adjust the stroke and tighten the stop dogs. Over the next month or two it happened again. It was puzzling. We put it down to Harry's age and the onerous night work.

I noticed that Harry, carrying a blue bottle of Bromo-Seltzer, made a trip to the john shortly after twelve each night. Finally, it dawned on me that the planer table had both times fallen off after one of these trips. One night I followed him and watched. First he washed his hands. Then he unscrewed the cap of the Bromo-Seltzer bottle and drank the contents. I caught the unmistakable scent of whiskey and the mystery was solved. Harry was a good old man and, aside from his occasional memory lapses in regard to the stop dogs, a wonderful machinist.

Harry was not alone in having a taste for whiskey. Luke, a quiet man at the last bench, had a thirst on him, too. In the cool dawn he often picked his way to the Blue Moon Cafe for a morning wet. Sometimes, in need of beer money, he offered to sell me one of his tools. I was needing more tools as I went along, so I usually bought. I'd offer it back to him next day for the same price, but he always refused, saying, "A bargain's a bargain."

Vermont workers never enjoyed much benefit from unions in those days. In most towns they were nonexistent or hadn't yet come up to strength. The one-armed man approached me one night and inquired softly if I'd like to join the machinists' union. I said I certainly would and he fixed me up with a dues book. The company was against the union and paying one's dues was a clandestine operation. You put the money between the pages of the dues book and slipped it to the steward when no one was looking. He stamped the back and slipped it back the same day.

The toolroom was only a small part of the factory complex. Though we had our share of characters, we were fairly quiet compared to the main assembly floor where Slim used to work. There were always a few, like Slim, who couldn't seem to settle in. Others sometimes adapted with help from their workmates.

One chap—the men nicknamed him Speed—aimed to be first out the door at the end of shift. Right after lunch each night, he put his jacket and lunch pail on a pile of heavy steel plate by his bench where they'd be handy in the morning. A split second after the whistle blew, he'd take off running, scooping up his jacket and pail as he flew by to be first at the time clock.

After awhile the other men got a little sick of watching him. After lunch one night they got the boss to send him off on a long errand. Then they welded his lunch pail to the steel plate, exactly where he'd left it. Word spread fast and just before shift time that morning, anyone who could legitimately do so made it his business to be hanging around the area. True to habit, Speed sat waiting and fidgeting with his time card. The instant the whistle let go he was passing his coat and pail at high speed. His hand, clawlike and accustomed by long practice, shot unerringly downward and closed tightly round the handle of his lunch pail. Those nearest him afterwards swore that Speed's arm stretched like a rubber band until his grip failed and he went tumbling down the floor. Next day, and thereafter, he was well back of first place when the morning line formed at the time clock.

Later, an uncouth individual who had never been properly toilet trained, was hired on the assembly line. Instead of walking down to the johns to urinate, he went off to a dark corner behind his work station and pissed on the dirt floor. He was quickly tagged with the name Dirty Sam.

Considering it was high summer and hot, that corner of the shop soon became a noisome place. Muttered oaths and threats had no effect on Sam's unpleasant sanitary habits. When they could stand it no longer, the others decided one night to take matters into their own hands.

"You want it stopped?" Charlie Matson said. "Leave it to me. I'll fix the bastard!"

Charlie hid a sheet of copper under a thin layer of dirt in Dirty Sam's private pissoir. Then he wired it up to electricity. That night, true to his established custom, Dirty Sam disappeared into the darkness of his corner. Suddenly there was a piercing scream and he staggered out clutching himself.

"By God, I hope it sterilized him!" was Charlie's only comment. "Prob'ly did, too, 'cause I give him a damned good jolt."

Sam never went near that corner again.

159

The shops were not the safest places in the world to work. Some of the machines were so large their operators had to stand on foot-high wooden platforms to handle the controls. Each had a chainfall suspended above it for hoisting heavy work into place. One night a chainfall let go, driving the machine operator through the platform floor and killing him. Another night a woman running a drill press forgot to put her cap on. Her long hair got caught in the spindle and she was scalped before anyone could help her.

The days wore on to fall. One night I looked up at the golden crescent of moon just visible through the skylight, then at the gray pallor of the men I had come to know and like. Many of them had gone out of their way to help me get started. They had worked, in their rough drab factory clothing, at the same repetitive tasks for most of their lives; for them the bright days were made for sleeping away. I thought of Nate, a man who had spent years with a mill file, its end ground to a sharp edge, endlessly scraping minute shavings from machined surfaces till they were dead flat—in the process cutting patterns in the gleaming steel till it looked like watered silk. Of Luke, the quiet, middle-aged alcoholic, patiently and carefully reaming holes, tapping threads, fitting sliding parts, for night piled upon night—for how many years? Were there any besides ourselves who truly knew and appreciated their painstaking work? I thought not. I made up my mind that nights were for sleeping and when I went home that morning I spent the whole day fishing. That night I gave notice.

Christmas

After I quit the machine shop I was at loose ends for a couple of weeks. It was partridge season and I spent a lot of time in the woods hunting. Then I thought I'd see if I could get taken on again at Twin State Fruit until I decided what I wanted to do next. I was experienced, and they were short-handed, so I got a job driving truck and working around the warehouse.

A couple of days before Christmas my father asked me to help him make the company Christmas baskets. Each year Twin State gave a basket to every employee: a cornucopia overflowing with fruit, nuts, vegetables, Italian specialties, a turkey, and lots more. It took us the whole of the first day to put them up. As things turned out it took all of the next day to deliver them. Dad and I loaded the baskets in a panel truck that morning and got through the Anglo part of the delivery pretty quickly. People asked us in for a polite drink or perhaps a cup of coffee and after an exchange of good wishes we left.

But when we reached the South End early in the afternoon, the pace of our progress became scarcely perceptible. Christmas, among White River Junction's Italians, was a well-celebrated festival. For us to carry the baskets into the jovial atmosphere of those Italian homes on such a day and leave after one drink would have been unthinkable, an insult to the house. Seated in the living room, we chatted with the men while the women made spaghetti and ravioli in the kitchen. We ate bread and cheese with hot milk and coffee. And we sampled an array of alcoholic drink that ranged from strong, homemade Dago Red to grappa, locally distilled from the skins and pressings of winemaking.

When the cork was drawn from a bottle of grappa you could see the smoke come off it. A drink of great authority, it was imbibed in serious amounts only by those who enjoyed living dangerously. Everyone else took it in tiny glasses as a ceremonial drink to mark the great occasions of life. In between these two distinctly Italian drinks we put down a variety of whiskies of which I best remember Old Overholt. It was not quite as strong as grappa but it was close. With the liquor we were offered, and expected to eat, antipasto, pasta dishes, roasted chestnuts, and imported Italian candies and cookies. Toasts were offered and returned. Often, someone in the family played the accordion and people sang while the others talked.

The day ended long after dark when I drove the truck on a weaving course through the falling snow to the company garage. We had a mile to walk in the freezing cold, which sobered us up some before we got home for our own Christmas Eve. The memory of that day is a fragrant one; each year, at Christmas, I think of it.

Postscript

Often, people younger than I are surprised I can recall the events of my childhood days so clearly. And I am puzzled when they tell me they cannot do so for themselves. If this is indeed true, perhaps one reason for it is that when I was a boy we lived much by the natural rhythms of the year and less by clock time. Time worked differently for us, and the events of our lives tended to stick in the mind.

But there is surely a second reason. As the folkways of a society like the one I grew up in begin to disappear, some members recognize their value as tradition bearers. When I was a youngster such people answered the questions a boy will ask. Often they pointed out questions I would have asked had I known more. From them I got stories and traditional lore. I thought of them as a special and unique breed, and I practiced the storyteller's trick of putting away in my head much of what they told me.

Over the last forty years the emergence of a post-industrial world has disrupted the fabric of life in the northern hemisphere beyond anything the world has known. Despite a long list of undoubted benefits of technology, there have been fearsome consequences. One is that we have become parasites on our own technology. Like a genie newly escaped from its bottle, technology has taken on a will and direction of its own.

The ripple-effect of this upheaval penetrates every backwater of the planet where enclaves of traditional peoples linger. It is killing these fragile cultures as surely and swiftly as a deadly virus. The peasantry of Europe, nomadic peoples in the mountainous places of the earth, South African bushmen, and the highland Yankee are but a tiny fraction of those whose days are numbered. All will vanish because they are different—and they are in the way.

The stories in this book were written partly out of a sense of nostalgia. But beyond that I have wanted to convey some feeling, however slight, of what it was like to live in the richness and diversity of a small, local culture still in contact with its past.

Now, it takes a native's eye to discern and give meaning to the scattered remnants of the world I grew up in. Woods laced with the stone walls of abandoned farm neighborhoods, the tumbled ruins of mills beside breached dams, old houses and barns, the derelict trackage and buildings of railroad yards—these are little enough with which to bridge the gap to an utterly different way of life whose lodestars were self-sufficiency and centuries-old traditions.

Goodbye Highland Yankee was designed by Michael McCurdy.
It was typeset in Times Roman by Dartmouth Printing Company.
It was printed on Lakewood, an acid-free paper, by BookCrafters.